HOLY HABITS

HOLY HABITS

A WOMAN'S GUIDE
TO INTENTIONAL LIVING

Mimi Wilson
AND
Shelly Cook Volkhardt

NAVPRESS

Discipleship Inside Out™

Discipleship Inside Out™

NavPress is the publishing ministry of The Navigators, an international Christian organization and leader in personal spiritual development. NavPress is committed to helping people grow spiritually and enjoy lives of meaning and hope through personal and group resources that are biblically rooted, culturally relevant, and highly practical.

**For a free catalog go to www.NavPress.com
or call 1.800.366.7788 in the United States or 1.800.839.4769 in Canada.**

© 1999 by Mimi Wilson & Shelly Volkhardt
All rights reserved. No part of this publication may be reproduced in any form without written permission from NavPress, P.O. Box 35001, Colorado Springs, CO 80935.
www.navpress.com

Wilson, Marilyn S.   1946–
    Holy Habits : a woman's guide to intentional living / Mimi Wilson and Shelly Cook Volkhardt.
        p.   cm.
    Includes bibliographical refrences.
    ISBN 1-57683-115-9
    1. Christian women—Religious life.   I. Volkhardt, Shelly Cook.
    II. Title.
    BV4527.W555   1999
    248.8'43—dc21   99-41452
                                                                                                CIP

NAVPRESS and the NAVPRESS logo are registered trademarks of NavPress. Absence of ® in connection with marks of NavPress or other parties does not indicate an absence of registration of those marks.

ISBN 978-1-57683-115-1

Cover Designer: Dan Jamison
Photo by Bruce Forster/Tony Stone Images

Some of the anecdotal illustrations in this book are true to life and are included with the permission of the persons involved. All other illustrations are composites of real situations, and any resemblance to people living or dead is coincidental.

Unless otherwise identified, all Scripture quotations in this publication are taken from the *HOLY BIBLE: NEW INTERNATIONAL VERSION* ® (NIV®). Copyright © 1973, 1978, 1984 by International Bible Society. Used by permission of Zondervan Publishing House. All rights reserved. Other versions used include: the *New American Standard Bible* (NASB), © The Lockman Foundation 1960, 1962, 1963, 1968, 1971, 1972, 1973, 1975, 1977; *The Message: New Testament with Psalms and Proverbs* (MSG) by Eugene H. Peterson, copyright © 1993, 1994, 1995, used by permission of NavPress Publishing Group; and the *New King James Version* (NKJV), copyright © 1979, 1980, 1982, 1990, Thomas Nelson Inc., Publishers.

Printed in the United States of America

6 7 8 9 10 11 12 / 13 12 11 10

From Mimi:

*To Calvin, my husband, who has
called me to spiritual excellence.*

*To Kurt and Lori Wilson, Tom Trinidad and Kyndra
Wilson, and Kevin, my children by flesh and by
marriage, who have been fellow travelers in the
journey toward a deeper knowledge of God.*

*To my grandchildren, whom I pray
may join the others in a deep thirst for God.*

From Shelly:

*For my beloved husband, Glen, and our boys,
Carl and Culver. I need you and love you always;
may we continue to grow together in our Lord.*

*For Norm and Muriel Cook, my dad and mom.
You set me on the path toward Him; my love and
admiration for you knows no bounds.*

Contents

S E C T I O N   O N E

OUR PART: Making Him Our Daily Focus

S E C T I O N   T W O

HIS PART: Changing Us from the Inside Out

Acknowledgments

To LIZ HEANEY, our editor, we express our deep thanks and gratitude for helping us solidify the direction of this book. We also thank many others who have aided and encouraged us in many different ways: Hope Anderson; the Bible study group in Vail: Marge Black, Margie Stephens, Angie Stevens, Susan Sisti, and Judy Phillips; Mrs. Carter, Linda Dillow, KathyJo Estes, Carolyn Eumurian, Wendy Graumann, Andy and Kathy Howell, Barbara Odom, Cherith Rydbeck, Karen Schmidt, Miriam Schoenig, Becky Sims, Kay Talbot, Alice Tate, Bentley Tate, Mr. Tokatloglou, Denise Vezey, Kent Wilson, Julie Witt, and Milei Yardley.

Dear Reader

I write this in the wee hours of the morning. My family is still tucked in their beds, sleeping soundly. I've poured a cup of coffee, lit the candles, and spent some time in prayer. I knelt at the same couch, in the same place where Mimi and I have prayed countless times over the years. We have seen God move the hearts of kings and paupers for His kingdom as we've knelt before Him. God has answered powerfully. We've seen babies born, entire ministries come forth, land provided, and sickness healed. The list of answers is unending. We have watched the mystery of the change that took place in our own lives as a result of spending so much time with our God.

Our friendship began over thirteen years ago. Mimi had come to Ecuador with her husband, Cal, and their three children to serve as missionaries. My husband, Glen, and I had the key to the house where they were to live for the first six months. It didn't take long for Mimi and me to realize that we were, in the words of Anne of Green Gables, "kindred spirits." Sometimes when we talked about the way we felt, the other would nod her head in astonishment. (We are both quite unique and, apart from members of our families, we had never met anybody with such similar reactions!)

We soon learned that we had other things in common. Mimi is a third-generation missionary. She grew up in Africa where her parents and grandparents served for many years. I am also a third generation missionary; I was born in Taiwan where my parents were missionaries and my grandparents before them served God in China. We both love being wives and mothers. We use our homes as a platform for ministry. We each have a tremendous capacity for enjoyment and a good laugh, and we love to have our lives spiced up by wonderful adventures, and even mishaps.

But what drew us to each other, above all else, was our passion for ministry and our deep desire to know God. Mimi taught a large group of English-speaking women and started four different projects to help meet the needs of the many handicapped children in Ecuador. I was involved in a large program of teaching the Scriptures to upper-class Spanish-speaking women. We began to pray together on a weekly basis, and as we met, we "spoon fed" one another. Mimi and I shared with each other the riches that God was teaching us as we prepared to minister to the women in our worlds. The truths we learned during those hours took firm hold within our hearts.

Mimi had already coauthored *Once-A-Month Cooking* when she came to Ecuador. I'll never forget the day we began to talk about the project that resulted in this book, *Holy Habits*. Mimi had struggled with dyslexia all her life, but she never let it stop her. In fact, what was thought of as a weakness became a strength. She learned to rely on others to help her in that area. One day, I offered to be her teammate in writing the truths found in the following pages.

Mimi and I are two of the most nontechnical people alive, but we are grateful for the technology that has allowed us to communicate and to write this book together even though Mimi and her husband have returned to Colorado. We've learned to send e-mails and talk via the Internet. Most of what we've accomplished has been done long-distance, but despite the miles, together we have met at the throne of our Lord, seeking His direction for what you hold in your hands.

Much of what you will read came out of our times of "feeding" one another. In order to avoid confusion, I have written everything in Mimi's voice, weaving both of our experiences and lessons from God into the fabric of the text. It gives me great pleasure to give my friend voice in this way.

Flowing throughout these pages is the living, moving, loving character of God, who calls each one of us to Himself. Section one explores who God is and how we can develop "holy habits" that will help us look on the character of God, fall in love with Him, and keep Him as our focus. Section two explores how, as we learn to look to God, He transforms us deep in the secret part of our souls by His grace, and gives us the power to do those things that are unnatural to us. As we make God our focus, He transforms our minds, our hearts, and our souls; He changes us from the inside out.

At the end of each chapter are questions to use for individual or group Bible study, which are designed to help you look into God's Word and process what you have learned about Him in that chapter. Our hope is that you will become more intimately acquainted with Him and excited about who He is to *you*. At the end of the book is a recommended reading list of the books that have helped Mimi and me gain a deeper knowledge of God.

Our prayer is that you will become so captivated with who God is that your heart will cry out, "What can I do in my relationship with such an amazing God?" His answer to you will be, "Look to Me, love Me, abide in Me, and I will show you."

Come with us as we journey toward holiness by looking to the Author of it.

SHELLY COOK VOLKHARDT

CHAPTER ONE

A Wake-Up Call

T HE MORNING OF MY THIRTIETH BIRTHDAY I* DETERMINED NOT to waste any more time. I looked in the mirror, wondering where my twenty-ninth year had gone. My face and body were beginning to show the signs of age, and that's not all! My mind was no longer as sharp as it had once been. I could no longer remember a simple phone number without writing it down. (Now I can't even remember where I put the paper!) I was used to feeling invincible. Time was passing much more quickly than I'd ever dreamed—what had I accomplished?

I had certainly been busy. I had three small children, my husband, Cal, and I had survived his medical school education and residency, we were settled in a lovely home, and Cal's medical practice was thriving. But I was rushing headlong through life, merrily checking things off my to-do lists. If you had asked me, I could have told you all about the things I was doing, but nothing about who I wanted to become. Common folk wisdom summed up my strategy to this point: "If you aim at nothing, you'll hit it every time."

I had seen the ardent love that my parents and grandparents had for God, and I had grown up within the circle of their godly passion. When I would awaken before dawn as a child, I could see the dim light of kerosene lamps coming from under my parents' bedroom door. I heard the murmur of their voices as they prayed. I so admired and loved my parents, and I wanted a relationship with God like theirs. How I wished I could sit down as an adult and talk with them about my questions! I wanted to ask them how they had grown to love God with such passion. But the limited phone service in their remote location in Africa made communication with them next to impossible.

I was looking for a pool of wisdom to tap into for my life plan, and I wanted to surround myself with examples of godliness that I could emulate. I believed that godliness was a set of behaviors, and that if I just did what my parents and other godly people did, then I too would have a deep love relationship with God.

Because I couldn't talk to my parents, I decided to take a couple of years to study and talk with other people, especially the elderly. They had already lived through most of life's passages. What could they tell me about what they had learned? For two years I bundled up my children each week and visited nursing homes, seeking to glean wisdom from those with experience. I asked the same questions over and over: "Looking at your life from this side, if you could do it again, what would you do? Is there anything you would change?"

During that two-year period, I also analyzed my own life. I got a notebook in which to chronicle conclusions, insights, and lessons. I did a study of how I was using my time and what I was thinking about. Although I had given my *life* to God, somehow I still thought of my *time* as mine. But a lifetime is made up of minutes either used purposefully or wastefully. What I was doing with my time now would make a difference in where I was at the end of my life. I began to see that time was a gift from God's hand. How could I best use this gift?

Through my time study, I identified areas where I was

wasting time. Meal preparation, I discovered, consumed many hours a week. Out of that time study came the cooking method that I describe in the book I coauthored called *Once-A-Month Cooking*. Now I cook one day for the entire month, and I've cut down the amount of time I spend grocery shopping and cooking, allowing more time for me to do the things I want to do.

What's in Your Hand?

Psalm 90 played a significant role in my thought life during those days. Moses was speaking to his people, affirming that the Lord had been their dwelling place for generations. The verse that became my daily prayer was "Teach us to number our days aright, that we may gain a heart of wisdom" (verse 12). I asked God, who has the perspective of eternity, to teach me how to make today count, to show me how to use the precious gift of each day purposefully. My heart's cry became "Teach me to number my days aright; I long to know Your perspective on this day. Don't let me waste it in insignificance. When I am in tune with Your heart, I am in tune with Your wisdom."

The last verse in Psalm 90 also captured my attention: "Establish the work of our hands." That was what I wanted. I wanted the investment of my life to pay dividends in the lives of those around me. I realized I could spend my life wondering where it had gone and where I was going, or I could make a conscious effort to spend it purposefully.

I learned from Moses, a favorite Bible character. He had been an example to me as I read of how his knowledge and understanding of God grew throughout his life. When Moses had his first recorded encounter with God in Exodus, God asked him, "What's that in your hand?" Moses replied, "A staff" (Exodus 4:2). It was a simple answer, but loaded with meaning. That staff was a significant part of Moses' life. It was probably nothing elaborate. Maybe it was only a heavy branch that he had smoothed out for his use. But it represented Moses' identity—

who he was, what he owned. God asked Moses to lay down the staff. For him it meant a releasing of all that he was into the hands of God. Only then could God really use him.

Through the events in my life, God was asking me the same question He had asked Moses. "What's that in your hand, Mimi?" As God also worked with my heart, I realized I needed to take an inventory of all that I was and how I was allowing God to use me. I knew that God was asking me to lay all these things before Him in obedience . . . to acknowledge them as gifts from Him as the eternal and sovereign God.

By the end of this two-year period, I had clarified my lifetime goals: I determined to become a woman of worship, prayer, peace, and wisdom. Contentment rounded out my list.

I now knew where I wanted to end up, but where was I to start? On a page in my notebook I wrote my list of goals. On the top of the next page I drew a horizontal time line. Age thirty-two was the starting point on the left. I was looking ahead to the end of my life, determining who I wanted to be when I got there. I wrote age eighty at the end of the line on the far right. At the rate I was going, however, I felt sure that I would lose my mind by then.

32   80

With my list of lifetime goals in front of me, I began to plot how to achieve them. If I wanted to become a woman of worship, I had to start worshiping God *today*. I set aside one morning a week for worship and prayer, a commitment I continue to this day. I thought that this would accelerate my spiritual growth, but the first morning I found that I didn't know what to do. My mind kept going around in circles. Worship was supposed to flow! Something was wrong . . . and then I realized, *I don't really know God! How can I pray or worship if I don't know God?* In my conversation with Him, I could go no deeper than my understanding of who He was. Mine was simply a surface conversation. I knew that godly people prayed and worshiped God, but when I set out to follow their example, God showed me how empty prayer and worship are when they aren't the response of a heart devoted to Him.

Holiness Can't Be Imitated

I had mistakenly believed that if I could come up with a plan and diligently follow it, then I would have the relationship with God that I longed to have. But in all my planning, I had missed the most important part. I had thought that godliness was following a set of behaviors; that if I simply copied those behaviors, I would be changed. But what I had seen in godly people was merely an earthly reflection of a holy God. *What I was seeking was the end itself — to be godly — without going through the process of being made holy.*

Scripture commands us to be holy. Leviticus 11:45 says, "I am the LORD who brought you up out of Egypt to be your God; therefore be holy, because I am holy." As believers, if we want to please God, we have no option but to seek to become holy.

I asked myself, *How can I obey God's command to be holy? How can I live God's life in the world?* I could see the effects of holiness in various people around me, but I had no idea what personal holiness required. I could imitate goodness in my behavior, but holiness could not be imitated. Holiness is a byproduct of our union with God.

I could develop the best habits in the world, but only a relationship with a holy God would make me holy. To try to be holy without knowing God would be like trying to write love letters without having a lover — or worse, writing love letters and never hearing back from your beloved. True worship and prayer can only flow out of a heart-response to His character.

The longer I thought about it, the more I recognized that my relationship with God had to be the basis for *all* my actions and lifetime goals. How could I claim Him as the one true God and not have a passion to know Him well enough to be changed by Him? If those around me could not see His impact on my character, I was sending the subtle message that I did not really believe in Him. I wanted my children and others to see that the most important thing in my life—my relationship with God—makes a difference in who I am and how I live.

Had I wasted those two years making all the lists and visiting with those people? No. God used it to show me that godliness was not something I could put on my to-do list. If my goal would become just knowing God, then He would take care of changing me into a woman of worship, prayer, peace, wisdom, and contentment.

I have chosen to make knowing God the foundation of all I am. My process of learning to know Him has been enriched by a long and careful study of His character, through His names and attributes. The closer I get to God, the more I fall in love with Him, and the more I am changed by Him. As the saying goes, I become like the company I keep. My goals and purposeful living have been built on the foundation of knowing Him. Nothing can diminish or take away all that I have gained. The journey has been rich and sweet.

Holy Habits: Keeping Our Focus on God

As I have spoken and talked with women around the world, I've met many who feel as I once felt . . . as if their lives are busy, and even productive, but without any real purpose. Unless we make knowing God the basis of all that we do, we *will* lack a sense of purpose. God created us to know Him, and until that longing is satisfied, we will feel emptiness, a sense of futility. As we get to know Him, He fills us with Himself.

When you and I focus on God, He also makes us holy. Holy habits are daily spiritual habits that help us transcend our circumstances and keep our focus on God. Our part is to make it a habit to know Him. His part is to make us holy.

For years I thought it was the habit that would make me holy, but nothing could be further from the truth. Let me repeat: *Our part is to make it a habit to know Him. His part is to make us holy.* Holiness is the result of the transforming work of the Holy Spirit. The habit is simply a vehicle that allows God to change us. Oswald Chambers says, "The one thing that keeps the conscience sensitive to Him is the continual habit of being open to God on the inside."[1]

Habits Imply Daily, Personal Action

Our prayer cannot be "Make me like Hudson Taylor, or Jim Elliot, or Amy Carmichael." We have to begin our own journey toward knowing God firsthand. Those who have helped us in our walk with God have only been role models, not the actual means by which we come to know Him. They are simply examples of what God does in a life that is focused on Him. We can be thrilled by the reflection of God we see in our mentors, but we must not forget that these individuals also did their part to allow God to make them into His image. Like me, many Christians seem to think that merely wanting to know God is enough—that the desire itself will ensure the end result. Yet we would never assume this in other areas of our life. For example, would we ever think that simply wanting to cook like Martha Stewart or play the piano like Linda McKechnie would enable us to do so? Of course not. We would recognize the need to put forth much effort to accomplish such skill. Similarly, we must take personal action to free God to work in our lives.

For an action to become a habit, it must be done regularly and repeatedly. Personal action is demonstrated through holy habits that help us focus on who God is in a practical way on a *daily* basis. Throughout this book we will be looking at holy habits that will help us keep knowing God as our daily focus. What our great God does in our hearts with our choice to get to know Him is what makes these habits holy.

Habits Imply Progress

If we walk in the presence of God each day, He will change us from the inside out. As we focus on Him, we will become more like Him, but not through any effort of our own. I cannot tell you how it happens, only that it does. As we trust in the character of the God Most High and let Him do in us what He wants, He will not disappoint.

A friend recently told me that for years she had struggled in her relationship with her mother. For weeks prior to a visit with her mom, she would pray that God would help her honor her mother and talk to her in a kind tone of voice. She would even visualize responding to her mother with kindness rather than anger or irritation.

"I spent an enormous amount of effort trying to behave toward my mother in a godly way. It was a lot of work," she told me. "But it never made a difference. No matter how much I prayed or how much I determined to be nice, I ended up responding just as I had since I was a child at home. I finally gave up trying and turned my attention toward forgiving her. But that, too, was impossible on my own effort."

She went on to say, "My view of God changed as I got to know Him better. At the same time, my responses toward my mother began to change. God had done a work in my heart. I realized that I had forgiven my mother and was even beginning to enjoy her. What is so extraordinary to me is that I had tried *so hard* to behave toward my mother in a godly way, but I couldn't pull it off. But when I focused on God, He changed me and in the process restored my relationship with my mother." How great is our God!

All we can do is focus on Him. When we do, He changes us from the inside out. He makes us holy.

Where Do We Begin?

When I set out on my journey to know God, the task seemed so daunting that I decided to take a year to study each aspect of

God's character as revealed through His names. In this book I will share with you some of what I have learned about God by studying His various names. But He is also so much more! Remember, you must go on your own journey toward knowing God; you cannot rely on what I or others tell you about Him—you need to know Him for yourself! The questions at the end of each chapter are there to help you do just that. Each chapter also looks at what kinds of holy habits might help you deepen your daily walk with Him, habits flowing out of a heart captured by God's character.

Will you join me in this journey of a lifetime? Will you join me in the journey toward knowing God?

P R A Y E R

Help us, dear God, to keep our conscience sensitive to You
so that we may walk holy before You.
We ask this for Your glory.
Amen.

Study and Discussion
Questions

1. Read Psalm 90. In some translations it is subtitled "A Prayer of Moses the Man of God." It's a fitting title for the theme of this book. As you read, look for references to God's character and make a note of them.

2. In your Bible or on a separate sheet of paper, note all the references to the shortness of life that you can find in Psalm 90. What light do these verses shed on the importance of living intentionally?

3. What are the prayers or requests that Moses makes of God in Psalm 90:12-17? Make a list of them.

4. Use Moses' requests in Psalm 90:12-17 as a guideline to write a prayer to God with your personal petitions.

5. Describe how God might answer the prayer "Establish the work of our hands for us" (Psalm 90:17) in your own life.

6. Read Psalm 92:12-15, in which the psalmist describes a goal for the end of life. Looking back at question three, how do Moses' requests reveal his end-of-life goals?

7. Read 2 Corinthians 2:14-15. Someone who spends time getting to know God will be marked by the fragrance of Christ. What does that mean in your life? List some ways that you can be the fragrance of Christ in your surroundings.

8. Psalm 46:10 talks about knowing God. What does it say that we can do to help us accomplish this? What can you do to make that a reality in your life? What does the verse say that He will be? How can you make that true within your heart?

9. Jeremiah 9:23-24 also deals with knowing God. What should be the "boast" of a believer? What facets of God's character are mentioned in verse 24? How do you see those being exercised today?

10. Mimi's lifetime goals are to know God and to become a woman of worship, prayer, wisdom, peace, and contentment. Do a word study on one of the goals on her list. Use a concordance or topical Bible to find five or more verses about that goal. Choose one that challenges you and write that verse below.

OUR PART:
Making Him Our
Daily Focus

CHAPTER TWO

Resting in the Almighty

Elohim

THE BLACKNESS OF THE AFRICAN NIGHT BLANKETED OUR VAN as Cal and I headed to the small mission hospital. Our sleeping children leaned against me like bags of flour. The driver believed that the best way to drive was to cover the shortest distance between two points. He took no notice of the enormous holes that threatened to swallow up the van. My father, a veteran missionary, had warned us about this road. He jokingly said that he had gotten his Ph.D. in driving through mud, but he would never drive this road if it had been raining. It had been raining all day, and the roads were like thick soup.

Our children were not even wearing seat belts, as our ancient van did not boast such "modern" devices. I could put my arms around them to comfort them, but I was powerless to protect them should our van tilt into one of the pits in the road. I was painfully aware that we could lose our lives on that muddy African road. I felt helpless and insecure. Panic gripped me. How big was my God? Could He be trusted in this situation? I needed a God who was outside my world, bigger than anything I knew in my humanity.

My journey toward knowing God had only just begun. In the darkness of that terrifying ride, I reviewed in my mind all that I had studied about God.

Almighty, All-Powerful; Always Has Been, Always Will Be

God wasted no time in unveiling His name to mankind. The first verse of the Bible reads, "In the beginning [Elohim] created the heavens and the earth." *Elohim* is a name for God made from combining two Hebrew words: *El*, which speaks of His power, and *him*, which indicates the plurality of God: the Trinity. When Scripture refers to God as Elohim, the writer is emphasizing that God is an all-powerful and transcendent God in which each facet of the Trinity shows His power. God defined the name even more clearly in Deuteronomy 10:17: "For the Lord your God is God of gods and Lord of lords, the great [*El*], mighty and awesome, who shows no partiality and accepts no bribes."

In Genesis 1:14 we read, "And [Elohim] said, 'Let there be lights in the expanse of the sky to separate the day from the night, and let them serve as signs to mark seasons and days and years.'" With those words, Elohim set earth time into motion, and ever since, time has marked everything in a human being's life: our bodies, our schedules, our thoughts, our health—everything. Although God created time, He does not live in it, nor is He bound by it. He is not limited by any of the things that bind us. He is over and outside of the realm of our time. He transcends time.

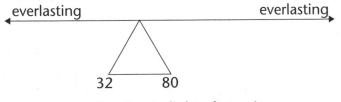

my timeline in light of eternity

I like how author and professor David Needham describes this aspect of God's character:

> When we reflect on the eternity of God, our tendency is to think that He has lived a long time. That He is very old. That He has been around for ages. But Scripture says something very different from that. It simply says that God *is*. Always has been. Never had a beginning. Never will have an end. He lives unfettered by time in any sense or any way.
>
> With God, there is no succession of moments. There is no future or past. He is one eternal *now*. He sees the whole of history—all of it—in action right now. He doesn't have to look back. He doesn't need to look ahead. He just sees it, with the end as much immediate to Him as the beginning.
>
> Years ago I watched a football game. Nothing unusual about that—except that it was projected at such an extreme speed that I saw the entire game in just three minutes. Players ricocheted up and down the field. Cheerleaders fluttered back and forth in the stiff breeze. The crowds boiled in the stands. Back and forth and back and forth—a blur of color—and it was over.
>
> If you asked me, "Did you see the game?" I would have answered, "Yes and no." It was all there, but I am built by God to comprehend a certain sequence of moments at a certain rate of passage. If you attempt to speed that up too fast or stretch it out too slow, I get frustrated. It loses reality for me. I'm not equipped to respond when such events are too compressed. I'm not able to live that way.
>
> But God is. God is eternal. In the infinity of His nature, He can see all the succession of moments of all of-time.[1]

Because God is outside of time, we can trust His timing.

We Can Trust His Timing—It's Perfect!

Noah did. The Bible tells us that Noah "walked with God"(Genesis 6:9), meaning that he *knew* God. He talked to God, and God talked to him. But the times in which Noah lived were wild and pagan. People had forgotten the wonder of creation and lived in wanton disregard of their Creator. God finally had enough and decided to destroy the earth (verse 13).

He gave Noah instructions to build a boat—a big one. The people at that time had probably never seen anything like it. When Noah began telling them that God was going to bring rain to flood the earth, they must have thought he was crazy. It had never rained before! Noah was caught between his God and his neighbors. It would have been easy to abandon the entire project and not be the subject of ridicule, especially as the years rolled by. But Noah did not waver in the face of laughter and derision. We are told, "And Noah did all that the LORD commanded him" (Genesis 7:5).

Noah knew that God was the Creator of time and that He was ruler over it. He understood that God knew the end from the beginning and that He would fulfill His Word in His time. God had told Noah, "I am going to bring floodwaters on the earth to destroy all life under the heavens, every creature that has the breath of life in it. Everything on earth will perish. But I will establish my covenant with you, and you will enter the ark—you and your sons and your wife and your sons' wives with you" (Genesis 6:17-18). Noah believed that God would do as He said . . . in His own time.

Because he trusted God, Noah was able to stand the ridicule of those around him and stick with the job he'd been given to do. From a human standpoint, building the ark was total folly, but the Almighty had spoken, and Noah looked to Him rather than man. Hebrews 11:7 tells us that Noah "became an heir of the righteousness which is according to faith" (NASB).

God's transcendence over time can be merely an intellectual

concept or it can be a truth that penetrates our lives. Because He knows the end from the beginning, we can trust Him. The future is uncertain to us, but it is no surprise to God, and we can rest in the knowledge that He has it in His hands. Our questions about our children and their lives are answered in His all-knowing transcendency. We can know peace because He knows the purposes for the heartaches and griefs of this life.

Is there something that you're longing for? Elohim transcends time. He knows even better than you when you have a need and what it is. As you get to know Him, you will start trusting His timing in every area of your life. This heart-awareness will allow Him to make deep changes in your perspective on life.

Helen was a beautiful young woman—charming and educated, although somewhat shy. She had accepted Jesus as her personal Savior as a child, and through her teenage years she learned to walk closely with Him. When she dated a boy, she would ask, "Lord, is this the one I am to marry?" Each time the answer came back, "No, not this one." Time passed. Helen never lacked for dates, but there wasn't one guy that was "right." As she entered her late twenties, Helen began to wonder if she would ever get married. Marriage and a family were the two things she had hoped for most in her life. For months she wrestled with God over the apparent discrepancy between His promise to give her the desires of her heart and the lack of a man to meet that desire.

Finally, she came to a crossroads. She would have to either yield herself to God or turn away from Him. She knew that God sees the end from the beginning. The time had come for her to put her faith in what she had heard. . . . Was she willing to trust God as Elohim? At night she tossed and turned, struggling to come to terms with what she was going to do with God. In the darkness of the early dawn, she at last laid her will under Elohim's, praying the prayer of yieldedness that David had prayed so many thousands of years before: "My times are in your hands" (Psalm 31:15). Peace flooded her soul . . . the peace that does not come from circumstances, but from knowing and trusting God.

The Creator's Fingerprints

Not only does the name Elohim reveal the transcendence of God, it also reveals the power of God as the Creator of all things. In Genesis 1 we read over and over again, "And [Elohim] said . . ." (verses 6,9,14,20,24). His very word brought on creation. In the Trinity, the *him* of *Elohim*, we have the Father, Son, and Spirit. In her book on the names of God, Kay Arthur states, "The *him* ending of *Elohim* is very significant, for it is a plural ending in the Hebrew that indicates three or more. . . . Thus, we see that each person of the triune Godhead had a part in creation."[2]

When I look at creation, I can learn about the constancy and faithfulness of God. Romans 1:20 says, "For since the creation of the world God's invisible qualities—his eternal power and divine nature—have been clearly seen, being understood from what has been made, so that men are without excuse."

God revealed Himself to Job by pointing to His creation to illustrate just how mighty and powerful He is. At the beginning of the book of Job, we learn that Job was a holy man. Even God considered him righteous. Satan asked God's permission to test Job to see if his righteousness was based on the fact that he had been abundantly blessed. Job's trials were incredibly difficult, all that he had was taken from him, and uncaring friends compounded his suffering. Throughout his interaction with his friends, Job continued to defend himself. Then God spoke to him out of a storm.

> "Where were you when I laid the earth's foundation? Tell me, if you understand. Who marked off its dimensions? Surely you know! . . . Who shut up the sea behind doors when it burst forth from the womb, when I made the clouds its garment and wrapped it in thick darkness, when I fixed limits for it and set its doors and bars in place, when I said, 'this far you may come and no farther; here is where your proud waves halt'?" (Job 38:4-11)

God asked Job questions to point out His handiwork in the world around him.

"Have you entered the storehouses of the snow or seen the storehouses of the hail, which I reserve for times of trouble, for days of war and battle? . . . From whose womb comes the ice? Who gives birth to the frost from the heavens when the waters become hard as stone, when the surface of the deep is frozen? . . . Can you bring forth the constellations in their seasons . . . do you send the lightning bolts on their way? Do they report to you, 'Here we are'? Who endowed the heart with wisdom or gave understanding to the mind? Who has the wisdom to count the clouds? Who can tip over the water jars of the heavens?" (Job 38:22-38)

When Job saw the power of God in creation, he said, "My ears had heard of you but now my eyes have seen you" (Job 42:5). He came to recognize his insignificance before God. By acknowledging God's power in creation, he submitted himself to His purposes and said, "I am unworthy—how can I reply to you? I put my hand over my mouth. I spoke once, but I have no answer—twice, but I will say no more" (Job 40:4-5).

As we seek to know God through His creation, the Holy Spirit whispers to our spirits and teaches us about Himself. As we are sensitive to His teaching, we can become acquainted with our Maker. In our society we are so bound by the written page and carefully explained television images that we easily forget that God is not limited by words. We can cultivate an awareness of what He wants to teach us about Himself in the glory of a sunset, in the power of a thunderstorm, or in the roar of an ocean wave. He is in all, He is over all, and He will show Himself to us because He wants a relationship with us.

Pachacuti was an ancient Inca ruler. The Incas of South America worshiped the sun god Inti. As Pachacuti studied the sun, he decided that Inti could not be the one true God and that it would be inconsistent to worship a part of creation if there was one god who created all. Pachacuti concluded that the sun god could not be perfect and all-powerful, as the Creator must be, because:

- Inti could not be universal if, while giving light to some, he withheld it from others (as shown by day and night).
- Inti was never at ease. He was always going around, revolving.
- Inti could not be all-powerful because the smallest cloud obscured him.

As he studied creation, Pachacuti came to the conclusion that the one true God would have certain characteristics that he did not see in the sun. He said:

> He is ancient, remote, supreme, and uncreated. Nor does he need the gross satisfaction of a consort. He manifests himself as a trinity when he wishes; . . . otherwise only heavenly warriors and archangels surround His loneliness. He created all peoples by His word . . . ordaining his years and nourishing him. . . . He is a bringer of peace and an orderer. He is in His own being blessed and has pity on man's wretchedness. He alone judges and absolves them and enables them to combat their evil tendencies.[3]

Pachacuti learned all this from the fingerprints of God in nature. God, through His Spirit, teaches the heart that is searching to know Him. This fifteenth-century Inca ruler wrote hymns that have been likened to the Psalms before the first European even set foot on the Americas. He looked from the creation up to the Creator, just as God beckons us to do.

Who Sustains the Life of a Tree During Winter?

The fall of 1995 was the first autumn season in ten years I had spent in the United States. In Ecuador, all we had was a rainy season and a dry season. The changing of the leaves amazed me. I had forgotten the majestic way the earth changes as it prepares for winter. I loved the variety of color. Outside my window was a magnificent tree that turned yellow. Why did I not grieve its death? Because it is normal; that is what is supposed to happen in the fall. The tree "dies" in preparation for the cold winter months. Who sustains the life of that tree during the winter months when it appears to be dead? Elohim, the Creator God.

When you put flower bulbs into the ground and watch the snow cover them in the winter, you have every reason to believe that they're going to come up in the spring. Why? Who sustains the life of those bulbs under the cold earth? Elohim. Who sustained the germ of life in peas that were found in Pharaoh's tomb two thousand years after they were placed there? When they were planted, the peas grew! God's sustaining power not only applies in the physical realm, which we see daily, but to every other aspect of life. There is no higher power than our God, in heaven or on earth, and His name is Elohim.

We see in Exodus 32 the power of His sustenance for the children of Israel even when they sinned by building the golden calf. The pillar of His presence was not removed. He continued to provide for them and their lives were spared. He could have removed His sustaining force, and they would have died. But He maintained His protection, thus sustaining their very lives.

Our daily lives are filled with the patterns that God spoke into being. The orbit of the earth around the sun, the pull of the moon on the ocean tides, the migration of animals, the molecular structure of DNA, and many other natural phenomena show us the intricate design of God. This incredible pattern was brought into being by the Word of God.

A *Newsweek* article entitled "Science Finds God" states that there are "signs that the cosmos is custom-made for life . . . if the constants of nature . . . were the tiniest bit different, then atoms would not hold together, stars would not burn, and life would never have made an appearance."[4] The article quotes physicist-turned-Anglican-priest John Polkinghorne, who feels that the fact that the laws of nature are so intricate "that [it] conspires to plant the idea that the universe did not just happen, but that there must be a purpose behind it."[5] *Newsweek* says that the occurrence of new discoveries "now implies to some scientists that there is a design and purpose behind the universe."

Many scientists are seeing that it's not a fluke that the world exists. Seventy-two-year-old Allan Sandage, a world-renowned astronomer, was a longtime atheist. He said that at age fifty, he was finally forced to recognize "that the world is much more complicated than can be explained by science. It is only through the supernatural that I can understand the mystery of existence."[6]

We have the great privilege of knowing Elohim, whose word spoke this phenomenal creation into being, whose plan is the pattern that many scientists are only beginning to recognize.

Several years ago, a friend of ours read a book on chaos theory and shared some of the ideas with our family. We were fascinated as he described to us the incredible concept of fractals—patterns within patterns that result from the application of random numbers to simple nonlinear equations. One such equation captivated us. As random numbers are plugged into the formula, then plotted on a graph as simple dots, no pattern is immediately discernible. But as additional random numbers are calculated, the pattern of a leaf begins to emerge. As additional numbers are run, it slowly becomes clear that the formula is producing the image of a fern. Is this the chaos of random numbers or the design of our Creator?

God's maintenance of order in our world, even in apparent chaos, can be a source of great comfort and security for those of us who seek to know Him. He cannot be thwarted by anything created. He will accomplish His purposes.

On a practical level, we see God's maintenance of order in the pattern of DNA, the chromosomal substance that stores genetic information. Now that man can isolate it, DNA testing has freed the innocent, identified the guilty, and helped make tremendous strides toward executing justice—all because there is a pattern that Elohim placed in His creation, an order that He sustains to this day.

The Word Became Flesh . . .

The apostle John wrote, "In the beginning was the Word, and the Word was with God, and the Word was God" (John 1:1). This Person, this Word, is Elohim. He was in the beginning. He was not *part* of this great creation, He was *before* creation. John 1:14 says, "The Word became flesh and made his dwelling among us." Here we learn that Jesus Christ is Elohim, God in the flesh.

To us, a word is something that is said or printed; it is flat, much like an empty glove. William Barclay quoted Professor John Patterson in his commentary on 1 John, saying, "The spoken word to the Hebrew was powerfully alive. . . . It was a unit of energy charged with power."[7] A word spoken was thought to take wings and live. The Hebrew concept of a word was as if it were a glove with a hand inside; it would grow and take on shape and force. So in creation, God's Word was powerful action.

The Hebrew understanding of the living characteristics of a word had not changed when the apostle John wrote, "In the beginning was the Word." When I read this verse in Spanish, I got a better idea of the power of the "Word." In Spanish the verse reads *"En el principio era el Verbo."* *Verbo* means verb, which indicates action, life, and power. Elohim spoke, and creation came to life out of nothing. Even the most creative people have to begin with something. God started with absolutely nothing and formed the earth. He spoke it into being.

This great God became flesh: "The Son is the radiance of God's glory and the exact representation of his being, sustaining all things by his powerful word" (Hebrews 1:3). Elohim did not lose anything simply because He put flesh around Himself. Why would an eternal being become a baby? He chose to do this so we would know who He is. Jesus is completely God and He teaches us about Him. He is the ultimate fulfillment of the Hebrew understanding of a word having a life of its own. According to Colossians 2:9, Jesus is the "fullness of the Deity." Everything we see in the Deity, all that we see in Elohim, we see in Christ. He is all that God was, is, and will be: *complete!*

Making Elohim Your Focus

What does that mean for you? When we invite Jesus into our hearts, Elohim, the Creator of our time, the Creator of the universe, the Sustainer of all life, and the Maintainer of order, comes to dwell within you! Through Christ we can know Elohim and all other aspects of God's character. That is a wondrous truth.

My favorite commentator, Matthew Henry, expressed his awe this way:

> And it is certain that the greatest favor that ever was showed to the human race, and the greatest honor that ever was put upon human nature, were exemplified in the incarnation and exaltation of the Lord Jesus; these far exceed the favors and honors done us by creation and providence, though they also are great, and far more than we deserve.[8]

How can you make this truth more real in your life?

HOLY HABIT:

"Hook" yourself to His transcendence.

As I focused on God's transcendence and tried to understand what it meant for me, I came up with a metaphor from skiing. I see God's transcendence as the line on a ski lift. Just as chairs are hooked to the line on a ski lift, when I invite Christ to live within me, I "hook" myself to God's transcendence. I am pulled through life by the strength of that connection. I desperately need a powerful God in my life, especially because I don't know exactly where

I am going. As long as I am connected to Him and His power, I will get where He wants me to go.

When you know that God through Christ dwells within you, you can face disappointments or hardships with a new perspective. Glen and Shelly had yearned for years to have children, but couldn't. They had spent thousands of dollars. Life had been reduced to charts, temperatures, medication, and endless rounds of appointments. They had submitted themselves to humiliating tests, undergone surgeries, everything. The doctors couldn't agree as to why they couldn't conceive. Shelly felt like a ball being smashed up against a wall and thrown back, over and over. She had been torn apart by promises of hope: yes, there was every chance that she could get pregnant; and by words that brought despair: "endometriosis," "infertile," "small chance," and "extraordinary measures." No one could count the tears she had shed, often under the roar of the shower.

She heard one woman say that dealing with cancer had been much easier than facing the impossibility of bearing a child. Shelly's body was an inhospitable place for the very thing she ached for! "God, what are You doing?" she cried over and over again. A battle raged within her. Why would God give her the longing to be a mother and then not allow her to have a child? She thought at times that she could not stand the grief any longer.

One day, after months of weeping, frustration, and anger toward God, she stopped her self-pity long enough to look at Him. What did she know about God? She knew that He transcends time and that He knows the beginning from the end. The future is no surprise to Him. Even in apparent chaos, He has a design. He is Elohim, all-powerful Creator God. Who was she to question Him? With that realization, Shelly laid her will into Elohim's hands, trusting the One who sees over the span of time with His plan for their lives.

After many long years of grief and a series of miracles, God gave Shelly and Glen a beautiful child through adoption. It was as if the pain of infertility was wiped away the moment Carl was placed in her arms. The first time a smile curved her infant son's mouth, Shelly thought her heart would burst with joy! Tears slipped down her cheeks and onto the soft blue blanket in which she had wrapped the little boy. She took what she calls "a heart picture," recording for all time the sound, look, and feel of that moment. Elohim, in His knowledge of all, had met their heart's desire. He could be trusted.

HOLY HABIT:

LOOK FOR HIS FINGERPRINTS IN THE WORLD AND TELL OTHERS WHAT YOU SEE.

One way I remind myself of Elohim's power in my life is that I ask Him to show me His fingerprints in creation. I read *National Geographic* and other nature magazines with the anticipation of seeing more of God's work. I deliberately stop to thank Him for the marvels of the things I learn in those periodicals. Often, a nature film will be as much of an incentive to worship as a praise service. Not long ago we visited an aquarium, and my heart was full of excitement as we saw God's creation in the creatures of the ocean. Many of those things had been unknown to man until recently, but God made them for His pleasure. I praise Him for that.

I also asked God to help me be aware of the things He did for my personal enjoyment. I started noticing the pleasure that I felt after a good laugh and the beauty of the smell of applesauce in the making. I deliberately stopped to recognize those things that brought pleasure and thanked God for His presence in them.

Every time Cal and I learned something new about the intricacies of creation, we would bring it up at the meal table and discuss it with our children. We called it "Table Talk." (This exercise is so important to me that my friend Mary Beth Lagerborg and I wrote a book on the subject, *Table Talk.*) Talking about what you learn not only cements the truth in your own heart, but it can also teach your children about the character of God and His constancy as seen in the world around us.

HOLY HABIT:
Acknowledge His power.

Take time to think about the power of God. Thank Him for His strength. Whenever you hear of a strong ruler like Saddam Hussein or some historical figure, say to yourself, "But my God is stronger." Use words like "Awesome," "Almighty," "All-powerful," and "From everlasting to everlasting" when you talk about God with others.

HOLY HABIT:
Celebrate Elohim.

The view of a beautiful city in the morning sun or its dying light can be a reason to celebrate Elohim's creative work. Allow your heart to celebrate Him with whatever is at hand in creation around you.

One of our favorite vacation spots is nestled in the mountains. On a clear morning, the view from the top of one of the peaks is spectacular. If one of us wakes up early and sees that the sky is clear, he or she wakes everyone up and we jump into sweat suits and drive to the peak. There we stand in awe and watch as the rays of the early morning sun change the surroundings from a delicate pink to a bright golden glow. We worship our Creator God as we enjoy the fruit of His handiwork.

Other times we have driven to a clearing not far from our home and celebrated a full moon and a clear night with hot chocolate and doughnuts. On the car stereo, the "Hallelujah Chorus" plays in the background, expressing what we feel. During those times, we talk of many things, seeking to recognize the fingerprints of God in all that surrounds us.

Our family also has "Celebrate the Faithfulness of God" nights. We invite a good storyteller or a missionary to tell how God worked in their lives. Then we invite other families and ask them to bring their small children so they can hear of God's greatness, too. Each family receives a copy of two hymns as they come in the door: "O God, Our Help in Ages Past," and "Great Is Thy Faithfulness."

After sharing a meal or dessert, we all stand and sing the hymns together. Then we spend the rest of the evening enjoying the stories of God's faithfulness. We close the evening with a reminder that because God is unchanging, we can trust Him.

✳

I SAT IN THE ANCIENT VAN AS WE HURTLED THROUGH THE DARK African night toward what I thought was certain death. My mind went back to what I had been studying about God. I had learned that He is Elohim, Almighty and All-Powerful. That meant that the situation we were in was not beyond His knowledge. Because He is Elohim, He sees the beginning from the end. His timing is perfect. He sustains our lives and nothing catches Him by surprise. I realized that if God chose to take our lives on that muddy African road, it would be the right time. My arms did not loosen their grip on our children, but as I was reminded of the fact that Elohim knew exactly where we were and what awaited us, my heart relaxed. I could rest in Him.

P R A Y E R

Almighty and everlasting God, You made the
universe with all its marvelous order;
its atoms, worlds, and galaxies, and the infinite
complexity of living creatures.
Grant that, as we prove the mysteries of Your creation,
we may come to know You more truly,
and more surely fulfill our role
in Your eternal purpose; in the name of Jesus Christ our Lord.
Amen.[9]

STUDY AND DISCUSSION QUESTIONS

1. What do Job 36:26, Lamentations 5:19, and 1 Timothy 1:17 tell us about God? How can this make a difference in your life?

2. Read Psalm 102:24-27. God's reign over time and His creation are mentioned several times in the phrases of these verses. Rewrite each phrase in your own words.

3. How does God's reigning over time and creation affect your life? Write down a story from your own experience that illustrates the power of that truth.

4. Pachacuti looked at creation and was taught about God by His Spirit. Study Psalm 71:17, 1 Corinthians 2:12-13, and John 16:13. What can we learn from these passages about the teachings of God's Spirit?

5. In Hebrews 1:3 we read of God's sustaining power. What does it say He sustains? How does He do it? In light of what we've read in this chapter, what does this verse mean?

6. Look up Psalm 18:35, Psalm 55:22, Isaiah 46:4, and Isaiah 54:10. Who are these promises for? What does God promise? How has God sustained you in mind, body, or soul?

7. Newer and more powerful telescopes are probing deeper and deeper into outer space, revealing that the earth is a tiny speck of God's creation. "The Hubbell telescope points to one of the emptiest parts of the sky, focused on a region the size of a grain of sand held at arm's length, and has found layer upon layer of galaxies as far as its eye can see."[10] Meditate on the fact that God created this space by His Word and He fills it with His presence. What is your reaction to how God fills the infinities of space? Write a psalm or prayer expressing the awe you feel about that.

8. Give other examples of the phenomenal pattern of creation. Start looking in newspapers and magazines for illustrations of the pattern and share those articles with your family over a meal.

9. John saw someone in heaven described in Revelation 19:11-13. According to John 1:1, who was that? (Note: We find Him in the beginning of Genesis and at the end in Revelation.) Explain why the robe dipped in blood is such a powerful image.

10. In John 1:14, John says, "We have seen his glory." What do you think he meant? Give some examples of how the disciples saw His glory. How have you seen His glory?

CHAPTER THREE

Experiencing a Fulfilling Relationship

Yahweh

SHELLY HAD TRAVELED HOME FROM COLLEGE TO VISIT HER parents one weekend. Her relationship with her mom and dad was full of joy and respect, and Shelly felt wrapped in their love during her visit. While she was there, a handsome young man invited her to a movie. Shelly's father explained that he knew of no films currently showing that he would be happy about her seeing, but that because she was an adult, she should make her own decision about going.

As the lights darkened in the theater, she was glad that she accepted the invitation. Her date's attention was flattering, and she had been studying so much that it had been a long time since she'd had so much fun. As the movie started and the steamy plot unfolded, however, she began to understand her father's objections. But it would be so embarrassing for her to walk out! Shelly sat, wrestling with wanting to enjoy the attentions of her date and wanting to please her father, who loved her more than life itself.

Finally, she could not stand it any longer. She whispered to her date that she was going home and ran from the theater to call her father, who quickly came to pick her up. Shelly said that it was her father's deep love that made her want to please him. Her father's tenderness had called her to purity and had drawn her from the movie theater. Her relationship with her father was so loving—so special—that it shaped the daily choices she made in her life.

God, as *Yahweh*, wants to have the same kind of relationship with us.

Yahweh Reveals God's Heart

One of the first places God reveals His desire for a special relationship with us is in Exodus 3 when Moses encounters Him at the burning bush. Remember the story? Although most Hebrews lived as slaves to the Egyptians, Moses had lived as a prince in Pharaoh's household for forty years. Then one day he murdered an Egyptian for "beating a Hebrew, one of his own people" (Exodus 2:11). When Moses learned that someone had seen his crime, he fled into the desert in fear for his life. He lived there for forty years, tending sheep. One day Moses noticed that a bush was on fire, yet not burning up. When he went over for a closer look, God called to him from the bush.

Everything changed for Moses when God spoke to him out of the burning bush. The first thing He told Moses to do was to take off his shoes. Moses was standing in the presence of Holy God, and deep reverence was due Him. There Moses stood, barefoot and awestruck. He certainly couldn't have anticipated what happened next. God went on to tell him that He had heard the cry of His people, and He is concerned for their suffering. "So I have come down to rescue them from the hand of the Egyptians. . . . So now, go. I am sending you to Pharaoh to bring my people the Israelites out of Egypt" (Exodus 3:8,10).

All Moses could say was, "Who am I . . .?" A modern translation might be: "You can't send me! I'm just a shepherd! What do I know about leading an army to fight the Egyptians— I'm not the man for the job!"

Then he went on to say, "Suppose I go to the Israelites and say to them, 'The God of your fathers has sent me to you,' and they ask me, 'What is his name?' Then what shall I tell them?" (3:13). God's response to Moses was, "I AM WHO I AM. This is what you are to say to the Israelites: 'I AM has sent me to you. . . . The LORD, the God of your fathers—the God of Abraham, the God of Isaac and the God of Jacob—has sent me to you.' This is my name forever, the name by which I am to be remembered from generation to generation" (3:14-15).

God presented Himself to Moses as I AM or *Yahweh*. While the name Yahweh had been used before, it had never been used in this way. With this introduction, God stepped into an intimate relationship with Moses. The name Yahweh was a special name which signified the personal relationship God had with His people. To everyone else, God was known as Elohim, but the Elohim of Israel was Yahweh. Later on God said, "I am [Yahweh]. I appeared to Abraham, to Isaac and to Jacob as God Almighty, but by my name [Yahweh] *I did not make myself known to them* . . . I will take you as my own people, and I will be your God. Then you will know that I am [Yahweh], who brought you out from under the yoke of the Egyptians" (Exodus 6:2-3,7, emphasis added). By revealing Himself as Yahweh to the Israelites, God moved into a new, more personal relationship with His people.

By the time Moses and the Israelites reached the Red Sea, it was clear in Moses' mind who was on his side. The Israelites cried out in fear when they saw the Egyptians behind them and the sea before them. But Moses had changed! He did not question himself or God, as he had at the burning bush. Instead, he announced to the people, "Do not be afraid. Stand firm and you will see the deliverance [Yahweh] will bring you today. The Egyptians you see today you will never see again. [Yahweh] will fight for you; you need only to be still" (Exodus 14:13-14). Those are powerful words from a man who not too many months earlier had lacked confidence in himself as a leader. Moses was learning to put his trust in God rather than in himself.

The Lover of Our Souls

I remember the incredible joy of lying on the bed with each of our children as newborns. The sweetness of their breath and the softness of their skin were like food to me. Often I would lie close to their little faces and try to draw their breath into my lungs. And I longed to be able to fill them with all the knowledge and wisdom that I had gathered about life. My memory of the tenderness of those moments comes to me when I think about Creator God. God, in an intimate act, breathed life into Adam! The intimacy of breathing another's breath is reserved for a parent or a lover. God is Father and Lover, and He chose this very personal way to give life to us.

Only man, out of all creation, was formed in God's image. We are singular in relationship to Him. In Genesis 3:8-9 we have a picture of God seeking man. He walked in the garden, seeking communion with Adam and Eve.

After Adam and Eve had sinned, God came once again to the garden. He asked them several questions, one of which was, "What is this that you have done?" (verse 13). Eve's reply, in the original version, actually meant, "The serpent caused me to forget."[1]

What are some of the things that she forgot?

- That she was made in God's image
- That she had a relationship with Him
- That Yahweh would want only what was best for her

We don't know all the things that she "forgot," but her sad confession reminds us that today we also forget. It was much easier to sin against the Powerful One, the Strong Creator, than the One who had walked with her.

When we remember that we have a personal relationship with God who has sought us out, whose image we bear, we realize that every sin is actually against Him who loves us.

Not Just a Place but a Person

I read that a huge shrine was erected on the spot where it is thought that Moses met God in the burning bush. People chose to worship and reverence the *place!* My first response at reading that information was to feel a bit superior and condemning, but I soon realized that I am no different from those who built the structure around that little bush. At times, we also enshrine the spectacular, the symbolic, and forget that God wants a relationship. Moses' encounter with God at the burning bush shows God taking the initiative to reveal Himself to man by reaching out of eternity into earth time. That is what is important—the bush was simply a vehicle! Those who make yearly pilgrimages to the site of the burning bush have lost sight of God's message to Moses: "I AM today what I was with Moses. You can know me today as Moses knew me because I am always the same."

When people come to our home for dinner I love to ask them how they got to know God. For me, the fact that God, the I AM, has called thousands of people through the generations to Himself is the most incredible love story. His call to each heart is unique. It is intimate and personal.

Beatriz told me that she came from a large, influential family. They faithfully attended church and followed the rules laid out by their leaders. As a young girl she took pleasure in the rituals and regularity of worship. But as she grew older, she became dissatisfied. There had to be something more. She went to church each Sunday, alert for something that would quiet the upheaval in her spirit. One day, God revealed Himself to her. She said that it was as if someone had been in the room. She felt God's call to her. From that day on, Beatriz entered into an intimate relationship with her heavenly Father. She was surprised by the intimacy she began to experience. She continued at the same church, but now there was a new depth. Her heart was filled with joy in a personal walk with God. The rest of her family could not understand it, but God did. She walked hand in hand with Him!

Moses had also enjoyed that kind of intimate communion with God. Imagine how he must have felt when God told him he could not enter the Promised Land! He had labored long and hard, and he had faced innumerable difficulties, all with an eye to getting the Israelites to Israel. Of all people, he deserved to make it into the land. But God told him he would not set his foot on the soil of that longed-for place. By then, his relationship with Yahweh had come far. He knew that he could trust Him and His plan.

In Deuteronomy 34:5, we read that Moses died in Moab, on the far side of the Jordan River, and God Himself buried His servant. But it didn't stop there. In the New Testament, on the Mount of Transfiguration, smack dab in the middle of Israel, who joined Jesus? Moses! Yahweh brought Moses into the Promised Land in His own time (Matthew 17:3).

The Ultimate Sign of God's Pursuit of Us

Jesus' presence on the Mount of Transfiguration—indeed His entire life—was evidence of God's love to the world. In the New Testament we read that in Christ we find all the essence of the Godhead. So, where was Christ when Moses met the I AM at the burning bush? Jesus said, "If I glorify myself, my glory means nothing. My Father, whom you claim as your God, is the one who glorifies me. Though you do not know him, I know Him. . . . I tell you the truth . . . before Abraham was born, I AM" (John 8:54-58). Although elsewhere in the Holy Scripture, Yahweh is the Triune name for God, here we see Jesus saying that He is Yahweh. As a member of the Godhead, Christ is an eternal being. He was at the burning bush and at the Mount of Transfiguration a thousand years later. The fact that Jesus became a man and took on a body did nothing to diminish His deity, His eternality. The Jews understood the implications of what Jesus was saying, and it so upset them that they took up stones to stone Him!

Once again, through the person of Christ, we see Yahweh making a step toward us that we might have an intimate relationship with Him. Because our sin nature keeps us from communion with Him, He provided a way to heal that breach. Jesus' final sacrifice on the cross was made so that we could have a relationship with Yahweh. God made provision for us even when that relationship was broken through Adam and Eve's choice to sin.

We were created with an infinite longing in our hearts for an infinite God. As Pascal, the mathematician and philosopher said, "There is a God-shaped vacuum in the heart of each man which cannot be satisfied by any created thing but only by God the Creator, made known through Jesus Christ."[2] He could have placed that longing within us and walked away once we sinned and turned our backs on Him. But in His mercy and grace, God allowed a solution to our yearning through the provision that Jesus made. Jesus is our link to God; Jesus makes it possible for us to have an intimate relationship with God. He wants to dwell within us.

Masaquini was born far from any hospital, deep in the Ituri forest. Poor nutrition and the rigors of delivery, combined with other factors, contributed to her being born with multiple defects. While she was still a babe in arms, she was accidentally dropped and suffered further injury to her already-twisted body. As Masaquini grew older, the villagers with whom she lived shunned her. Because she could not be productive and support herself, she was a weight on the entire community and was made to feel that she was a burden. She did not feel welcome anywhere.

One day she dragged herself to where my parents were holding meetings. Her shriveled form and bent limbs made it difficult for her to breathe deeply. But she came because of a hunger deep within her soul. My mother was drawn to the corner where Masaquini was crouched. In answer to the pleading in her haunted eyes, my mother began to tell her of God's love and of His desire for a relationship with her. With the dawning of understanding that she could bear the love of God within her, Masaquini began to smile. Once she grasped the concept that even her bent form was a worthy dwelling for God, she finally found her place. Because of a relationship with Yahweh, she found worth and value.

Christ, who is Yahweh, wants a relationship with you; He dwells within you. When we know Christ as Yahweh and find our worth and value in Him, we are motivated to be like Him . . . to be holy as He is holy.

Called to Purity

Yahweh is holy: "Be holy because I [Yahweh] am holy" (Leviticus 19:2). He calls us to be holy. What is holiness anyway? Traditionally holiness has been understood as being set apart for God. Bible commentator William Barclay gives us a fresh perspective when he says, "The word for holy is *hagios* whose root meaning is different . . . the Christian is *hagios* because he is different from other men. The Christian is God's man by God's choice. He is chosen for a task in the world and for a destiny in eternity. The Christian is chosen to live for God in time and with Him in eternity. In the world he must obey His law and reproduce his life."[3] The Christian is meant to be different, to live God's life in the world.

In his book *Our God Is Awesome*, Pastor Tony Evans says that if we "are serious about walking with God, we have to understand who He is and who we are in light of Him." He goes on to say:

> God's holiness unlocks the door to understanding and making sense of everything else about Him. . . . God swears by His holiness (Psalm 89:35). Why? Because it is the fullest expression of His character, because it fully explains who He is. The Bible declares that God is holy in all of His being (Leviticus 19:2). Holiness is the defining point of God's character. At the heart of who God is, is His holiness.[4]

In other words, Yahweh's holiness is an integral part of His being. We read in Scripture that all aspects of Him are holy. God in His holiness is pure and perfect. When the Israelites praised God for their deliverance from the Egyptians, they cried, "Who among the gods is like you, [Yahweh]? Who is like you—majestic in holiness" (Exodus 15:11).

In *The Pursuit of Holiness,* Jerry Bridges says we are changed when we come to know God as holy:

> Because God is holy, He hates sin. . . . Therefore
> every time we sin, we are doing something God
> hates. He hates our lustful thoughts, our pride and
> jealousy, our outbursts of temper, and our rational-
> ization that the end justifies the means. We need
> to be gripped by the fact that God hates all these
> things. . . . We need to cultivate in our hearts the
> same hatred for sin that God has. The more we
> grow in holiness, the more we too hate sin.[5]

God's holiness puts our sin into perspective. To have a relationship with a holy God, we have to do something about the sin in our lives. Our sin is a barrier that keeps us from Him. When we accept His forgiveness of sin offered through the sacrifice of His Son on the cross, His holiness calls us to purity. "As we grow in our knowledge of Him," writes R. C. Sproul, "we gain a deeper love for His purity and sense a deeper understanding of His grace."[6]

When God commands us to be holy, He prefaces the command by stating that He is the Lord and He is holy. A great man of God, Andrew Murray, said, "There is nothing that God has that He does not want to give. It is His nature; and therefore, when God asks anything of us, He must give it first Himself, and He will. Never be afraid whatever God asks; for God only asks what is His own; what He asks you to give He will first Himself give you. The possessor, and owner, and giver of all! This is our God."[7] Only God can make us holy. He wants to make us holy.

When you and I maintain an awareness of God's holiness and the privilege of intimacy with Him, we have a compelling reason to run from sin. A college student I know told me of the challenges he was facing in the immoral environment of the secular university he attended. Many nights when he returned to his dorm, he found his roommate and girlfriend using the room. One time he walked in to find that several guys were passing a girl among them. She offered herself to him as well, but he turned and walked out of the room. Sometimes he stretched out on the floor in a friend's room or sat and studied outside his own door until the coast was clear. His roommate thought he was crazy and made fun of him. When I asked him what had kept him pure, he looked me in the eye and said, "I have committed myself to God. As a part of that commitment I plan to stay pure until marriage. I will not do anything to disqualify myself as a servant of God."

This young man had his focus on Yahweh and not on gratifying his physical desires. His life was markedly different from those around him because of the consciousness of his walk with a holy God.

The name Yahweh is so sacred to Jewish people that they do not dare say it out loud. They fear an inadvertent irreverence toward His holiness. Because they revere Him so much, they use only consonants to refer to His name, YHWH. I once asked a Jewish woman how she prepared for the Passover holiday. She told me that for six weeks prior to Passover, she cleaned every corner of her house. She even took a cotton swab to the baseboards. She explained that there must not be one bit of dirt or leaven in a Jewish home when Passover is celebrated because that represented sin and would disqualify the home from the presence of God. "You must love God incredibly to go to that extent to honor Him!" I exclaimed. She looked at me in surprise. "Love Him? You mean I would do this for love?"

This dear woman was motivated by her fear of the holiness of God and a blind following of tradition. Sadly, she had no understanding that she was created to have a personal love relationship with Yahweh. When we look at God's holiness apart from relationship with Him, it *is* cause for fear. But Isaiah 57:15 says, "Thus says the High and Lofty One who inhabits eternity, whose name is Holy: 'I dwell in the high and holy place, with him who has a contrite and humble spirit, to revive the spirit of the humble, and to revive the heart of the contrite ones'" (NKJV). When Yahweh's holiness is viewed from the safety of intimacy with Him, we see sin as He does and long to be free of it.

Always the Same

The name Yahweh not only tells us that God wants a relationship with us and that He is holy, it also signifies that God is unchanging.

The first time I read God's introduction of Himself as I AM, I was confused. I AM didn't mean anything to me! However, the longer I have lived with Him as I AM, the more I am filled with awe. The I AM never changes. God is always the same. His name is not I Was, or I Will Be. He is I AM. He will be I AM when tomorrow arrives and He was there as I AM yesterday. If you catch me on a good day, I might be pretty close to what I was the day before, but I will not be exactly the same. More hair will have fallen from my head and my wrinkles will be a bit more pronounced. You wouldn't notice over the course of days or even weeks, but if you had not seen me in a long while, you would definitely notice that I am *not* what I was! God isn't like that. He is always the same. There is freshness with Him continually. He is the life giver who lives in eternity in our time, which is past, present, and future, and He never changes. The closest we can come to His unchangeableness is in our relationship with Him.

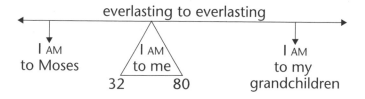

Helen came to me one day with her eyes glowing. "I've gotten a new glimpse of God that has shaken me to the core!" she cried. "I've been reading about the Israelites' journey across the desert and found myself wondering why God never did anything incredible for me like He did for them. They went from one miraculous provision to the next. It seemed to me that God is different now than He was then. But how could I think that when the Bible tells us that God hasn't changed? I asked God to show me why He doesn't do miraculous things in my life, if it was true that He hadn't changed. The answer came back so clearly! My lack of faith limits His freedom to do great things in my life.

"I have started asking Him to show me how to live with Him as the big God that He is. If only I could tell you everything that has happened since I prayed that prayer. I've never seen more prayers answered. I've been up against some things that were, to me, as big as the Red Sea, and God has parted them for me. He hasn't changed, but I sure have. I never again want to limit His freedom to work in my life!"

Making These Truths Real

What can we do each day to remind ourselves of who God is as Yahweh?

HOLY HABIT:
REMEMBER THAT HE IS A BIG GOD.

Make a list of those areas in your life in which you find it difficult to trust God. Then go to the Bible and find incidents where He worked in the areas of your weakness. On a 5" x 7" card, write the reference and a one- or two-word statement that reminds you of what He did. Go over it each day to remind yourself that He has not changed. He wants you to allow Him to work in your life. He is a big God. Ask Him to help you live with Him as a big God.

HOLY HABIT:
RECOGNIZE EACH DAY AS A GIFT BOX FROM GOD.

Each morning God reaches out of eternity, and gives us a gift: *today.* I used to think that my day was something that I invited God into each day. But the truth is, God is there already. I don't invite Him, He invites me! It is He who welcomes *me* into my day.

He is present with me today, He was with me yesterday, and He will be with me tomorrow. He is I AM.

This understanding revolutionized how I spend my time each day. *Will I use today to get to know Him better?* I cannot go back and relive the past, and tomorrow has not yet been given to me. Today is all I have. Both the future and the past are part of my eternity, but right now I am responsible only for today.

As I have learned to know God, I have learned that the gift of today is not to be taken lightly. As Yahweh, He is holy and is to be treated as such. My day is a gift from God, and I use it to reverence Him.

When I first began to practice the holy habit of viewing each day as a gift from God, I kept a special gift-wrapped package on my bedside table. It was the first thing that I laid my eyes on in the morning. I wanted a concrete reminder that the new day was a gift from the hand of God, to be opened and enjoyed. When the end of the day came, I spent a few moments reviewing the events of the day. Then I took what I had done that day, mentally placed it in the box, and offered it back to God. Every day I hang my box next to all the others on my eternity line, each representing that God was with me that day.

I have 52 years worth of package
hanging on my eternity line

This habit has become so ingrained in me that I no longer need the box as a reminder. But I continue to mentally go through this exercise. This habit of seeing today as a gift helps me to recognize God's loving gifts to me, and it encourages me to look for Him throughout the day. I have chosen to live purposefully by developing the habit of affirming His gift of each day and by fully recognizing Yahweh's presence in it.

Moses was eighty when he met Yahweh, and he became a

different man. Could it be that he was contemplating the fact that he had wasted eighty precious years when he wrote in his psalm, "Teach us to number our days aright, that we may gain a heart of wisdom" (Psalm 90:12)? Even if we start late in life, it is better to live with the purpose of knowing God for a week or a year than to live an entire life and not know God any better.

HOLY HABIT:

DISCIPLINE YOUR MIND.

Because time is so precious, I wanted to make a plan for how to best use my time. But first, I needed to have a better handle on where my time was going. I broke the day into fifteen-minute segments and used a timer to remind myself to make a note of what I had done and thought during that period. I was appalled by what I thought. I would hear a siren while vacuuming the house before Cal came home from work and would immediately wonder if he had been in an accident and was in an ambulance on the way to the hospital. What would I do if he were killed? How could I work with small children to care for? Who would watch them? Before long, I had worked myself up to a panic about how I would cope without Cal. By the time he walked in the door, I had his funeral planned and even knew what I would wear to it!

You would think I would have learned my lesson, but inevitably something would come along to carry me away again. I found a questionable lump on my body. Because my imagination is vivid, I'd jump to the conclusion that the lump was cancer and that I had only a few months to live. I would wonder who would come to my funeral and even worse, who Cal would marry! I would stew about it all day to the point that when Cal came home and asked how my day was, I would feel drained. Planning a funeral all day takes a lot out of you! But how could I tell Cal that I wondered who he'd marry if I died? He didn't even know about the lump. My mind was undisciplined in spite of the fact that I had invited the great and holy Yahweh into my life.

First Peter 1:13 says, "Therefore, prepare your minds for action." Peter makes this call for mental discipline, and then goes on to state that we are to be holy. A disciplined mind helps us keep our focus on Yahweh. I felt that my lack of mental discipline was so critical that I continued my practice of setting a timer every fifteen minutes for a while. Every time it rang, it was a reminder to check my thoughts and ask God to help me bring them into line.

HOLY HABIT:
DWELL ON HIS LOVE FOR YOU.

Each morning I trained myself to greet the Lord first. My first thought is "Good morning, my Father." And my last thought at night is "Good night, my Lord." I have also read the prayers of others that were written for morning and evening as aids to help me focus on Him. I try to notice things that show God's love for me. I have done a word study on the love of God and written out some of the verses that spoke to my heart as reminders of His love.

❋

HE IS A HOLY GOD WHO HATES SIN AND CANNOT LOOK ON IT. YET, He seeks relationship with His creation; He longs for intimacy with you! Scripture records the love story between God and humankind, a love story full of passion and romance, a love story of how God woos us into relationship with Him. Our God has been called the "Hound of Heaven" because He relentlessly pursues us. He is a lover who is not easily put off. . . . He comes back again and again, calling us into relationship with Himself. He has no need of us. He simply wants us. Will you draw near to Him?

P R A Y E R

Oh Lord, enlarge and purify the mansions of our souls
that they may be fit habitations for Thy Spirit,
who dost prefer before all temples
the upright heart and pure.
Amen.[8]

STUDY AND DISCUSSION QUESTIONS

1. In John 17 we find Jesus' intercessory prayer. He prays "keep them in Thy name" in verses 11-12 (NASB). How do you think the name Yahweh "keeps us" in the world?

2. Read Exodus 3:14, John 8:58, Hebrews 13:8, and Revelation 1:8. Explain how the truth of these verses is linked together.

3. In Hebrews 13:8 we read that Jesus is always the same. Look up Malachi 3:6 and Hebrews 1:12. How should the truth of these verses impact your life?

4. Read Numbers 23:19, 1 Samuel 15:29, Isaiah 40:8, and Isaiah 40:28. Make a list of all the things found in those verses that do not change about God.

5. The Jewish woman cleaned her house for Passover, but she didn't understand that it could be done out of love. What do you do that is simply for the love of your Lord?

6. Read Psalm 99. Note all the times it refers to God as holy. Make a list of what Psalm 99 says we are to do in the face of His holiness. What can you do that reflects what you know of God's holiness?

7. Read the following verses and make notes on how the holiness of God is mentioned.

   - Exodus 15:11
   - Leviticus 11:44
   - 1 Chronicles 16:10
   - Isaiah 6:3
   - Mark 1:24
   - Luke 1:49
   - John 6:69

8. Read Psalm 103:1-14 and make a list of God's works on behalf of His people and His characteristics. Where have you seen God work in your life this week?

9. Review Psalm 103:12, then read Isaiah 38:17 and Isaiah 43:25. Write a statement about what you understand that God does with your sin based on these verses. If this is true, how does it make you feel?

10. Read Jeremiah 31:3. God makes a strong statement in this verse. Find at least one more verse that speaks about His love for us (use one of your favorites, consult your concordance, or use the cross-reference feature in your Bible). Compose a love note to God, writing your response to His declarations to you in Jeremiah 31:3.

CHAPTER FOUR

Enjoying God's Provision

Yahweh-Jireh

*D*URING THE GREAT DEPRESSION, A COUPLE WITH THREE children felt God's calling to serve as missionaries in Africa. They had no money to finance a move to the mission field, but they did own their small home. If they could sell it, they would have the money they needed . . . but who would buy it? The economy was at an all-time low and people did not have the money to buy real estate. But they put the house on the market, trusting God for a miracle.

One evening as the family was on their knees, once again asking God for the sale of their home, He spoke to a woman across town, telling her to buy their home. She got on a bus, clutching her purse in her hands, and rode over to their house. When she arrived, she saw the family get up off their knees, and she rang the doorbell. "God has told me to buy your house so you can go to Africa." The lady drew money from her purse and made a down payment. The family was thrilled with God's provision! With the money from the sale of their home, they had the means to go to the mission field.

The daughter was sixteen when her parents moved to Africa. After a few years, she returned to the United States to attend Biola College. While there, she met a handsome young tennis champion who had played against well-known tennis player Bobby Riggs. The two fell in love and were married. Soon after the wedding, the young woman discovered that the woman who had purchased her parents' home, enabling them to travel to Africa, was her new husband's great aunt!

Upon graduation from college, the newlyweds also moved to Africa where they worked as missionaries for fifty-two years. During those years of ministry, they lost their household several times due to major theft, political turmoil, and the elements. All their wedding gifts and most of their treasures were taken from them. When it came time for them to leave Africa, they had little to call their own, and retirement in the United States seemed daunting. It would have been easy to worry about where they would live and how they would eat. But they didn't worry. God had been providing for them all through their lives. He would again.

Shortly before they were scheduled to leave Africa and retire, word came that the great aunt had willed the couple the very house that had been sold to her to provide the parents' first trip to Africa! It was completely furnished, down to the linens, china, and crystal! That couple was my parents. When they arrived in the United States after all those years, possessing only the suitcases in their hands, they returned to the same house that my grandparents had sold when my mother was sixteen years old. God provided for my grandparents to go to Africa, and many years later, for my parents upon their return.

Our God is Yahweh-Jireh, the Lord Who Provides.

Provision Is Who He Is

Provision is a part of who God is. In Genesis 22 we read a familiar story in which God revealed Himself as Yahweh-Jireh and taught all mankind a lesson with far-reaching implications.

Abraham and Sarah had longed for a child. After many years,

they finally received the child God had promised. Isaac, whose name meant "laughter," brought great joy to their home. Abraham and Sarah raised Isaac with love and tenderness. Surely all their grief and agony was behind them; nothing could be worse than the pain of infertility that they had endured.

One night God called, "Abraham!" "Here I am!" replied Abraham. God said, "Take your son, your only son, Isaac, whom you love, and go to the region of Moriah. Sacrifice him there as a burnt offering on one of the mountains I will tell you about" (Genesis 22:1-2). Scripture tells us that Abraham got up early the next morning, cut enough wood for the burnt offering, and set off for Moriah with Isaac and two of his servants.

Moriah was a three-day journey. The long days of difficult travel, combined with the knowledge of what he had been asked to do, must have been wretched for Abraham. But the nights must have been even worse. In the tough times of life, the nights are the most excruciating. I can picture Abraham standing under the stars, searching the sky, straining to hear God's voice giving him new instructions. He must have had a thousand questions. God had waited until Abraham and Sarah were too old to have children naturally and then He had supernaturally provided Isaac. Why would He satisfy their longings after years of barrenness only to ask them to sacrifice Isaac? Had Abraham heard God right? Was he really going to be the father of many? Was God's promise to him real? Why had God sent them to Moriah? There were plenty of adequate altars and places for sacrifice right around Abraham's home, to say nothing of all the possibilities between there and Moriah! Abraham had no idea of the long-term significance of the location and why they had to make such a journey, but God had a plan He would reveal in His time.

Finally, on the third day, Mount Moriah came into sight. Abraham instructed his servants to stay with the donkey. He said, "We will worship and then we will come back to you." He left the servants there. The Bible says,

> Abraham took the wood for the burnt offering and
> placed it on his son Isaac, and he himself carried
> the fire and the knife. As the two of them went on
> together, Isaac spoke up and said to his father Abra-
> ham, "Father?" "Yes, my son?" Abraham replied. "The
> fire and wood are here," Isaac said, "but where is the
> lamb for the burnt offering?" Abraham answered, "God
> himself will provide the lamb for the burnt offering, my
> son." And the two of them went on together. (Genesis
> 22:6-8)

Abraham built the altar with a heavy spirit. He laid his only son on the altar and raised the knife to kill him. Only then did Abraham hear God's voice and see a ram caught in a thicket behind him. Abraham took the ram and sacrificed it as a burnt offering instead of his son, Isaac. "So Abraham called that place The LORD Will Provide" (Genesis 22:14).

What a thrill for both Abraham and Isaac! God had provided the perfect lamb for the sacrifice . . . but this is not the end of the story.

Years later, God directed Solomon to build the temple on the same mountain—Mount Moriah (2 Chronicles 3:1). Up until this time, the Israelites had been using the tabernacle as the place to offer their sacrifices for the forgiveness of their sins and as their place of worship. In His time, God allowed Solomon to build a beautiful, permanent temple on Mount Moriah, the same site where He had provided a lamb for Abraham's sacrifice. Once again, God had made provision.

Many Bible teachers and theologians believe that when God provided for Abraham's sacrifice, something far deeper than Abraham's heart-lesson and trust-test was in God's plan. He was looking *over* time far beyond Abraham and Isaac, and He was reaching down and providing *in* time. God did not choose Mount Moriah at random; in His omniscience He knew that the temple would be built there. God's provision of a ram for Abraham's sacrifice was a foreshadowing of *all* the sacrifices that would eventually take place on Mount Moriah once the temple was built there. He is Yahweh-Jireh, the God who sees and provides.

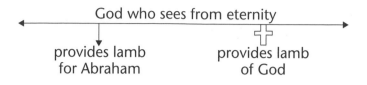

But, there is more.

Hundreds of years later when John the Baptist saw Jesus by the river Jordan, he announced, "Look, the Lamb of God, who takes away the sin of the world!" (John 1:29). John was announcing to the crowd that Jesus was from God; He was perfect, without blemish, and would be sacrificed for man's sin. We read of that sacrifice in Matthew 27. Once again, a Father leads His only Son up a mountain, and once again God provides a sacrifice . . . only *this* time God does not have a ram in the thicket. This time God sacrifices His only Son for the sins of humankind.

Powerfully, miraculously, Yahweh-Jireh saw and provided for Abraham's sacrifice. That alone would have been enough. But through Christ, God provided for the sins of man *for all time*. Up until then, the children of Israel had to make *ongoing* sacrifices for their sins. But "Christ died for sins once for all, the righteous for the unrighteous, to bring you to God" (1 Peter 3:18). From eternity, God could say, "I will provide a lamb for you now, Abraham. But I will not spare My Son, the One that I love. The Lamb of God will be slain one day so that *once for all, sin will be forgiven.*"

Revelation 13:8 says, "the Lamb that was slain from the creation of the world." This verse underlines the difficulty of comprehending the fact that God is not in time, nor is He bound by it. He exists in the past, present, and future while presiding over all time. Before the earth ever came into being, God knew that He would send Christ to the cross. It was God's plan before man was created or Adam sinned.

Yahweh-Jireh is the God who sits above time and can see the past and the future. He inhabits eternity. All time for Him is the present . . . and in His knowledge of the past and the future, He provides. The mental image I have of this is that God has a full storehouse of things that He wants to give me. But because of His perspective on time, He waits until the time is right for me. I could not contain all His kindness if He gave it all at once. I have to trust Him and His provision in my life.

Grace to Become Like Him

The God you worship is Yahweh-Jireh, the God who, in eternity, sees and provides. He declares, "Even to your old age and gray hairs I am he, I am he who will sustain you. I have made you and I will carry you; I will sustain you and I will rescue you" (Isaiah 46:4). In Romans 8:32-33, we are told, "If God is for us, who can be against us? He who did not spare his own Son, but gave him up for us all—how will he not also, along with him, graciously give us all things?" Those promises are for you.

All that we experience from the hand of God is a free gift. The Bible calls it grace—undeserved favor. To begin to grasp the extent of God's generosity to us, we need to break it down into sections. In the spiritual realm all is undeserved: our *salvation, justification, sanctification,* and *glorification.* Let's take a closer look at what these theological terms mean.

Salvation: The moment we accept God's gift of relationship with Himself through faith in the provision of Jesus, the Lamb of God, we are "saved." At that moment He gives us His Spirit and we become His children with the promise of eternal life. Salvation is by grace; it is unmerited.

Justification: Because we have accepted Jesus' sacrifice on the cross and we belong to God, He does not count our sinfulness against us. He imputes to every believer the righteousness of Christ. God sees us covered with the blood of Jesus Christ, which gives His people a right standing before Him. Our justification is given by God's grace and, therefore, is undeserved.

But God wants more for us. He wants us to be like Him, to be godly.

Sanctification: The next step is *sanctification*, the process of becoming like Christ. "You cannot do anything for your salvation, but you must do something to manifest it, you must work out what God has worked in."[1] Because of our sinful state, becoming Christlike will take you a lifetime; it is a long, slow process. We can be assured that the Holy Spirit will work in us every step of the way. We are just as unworthy of sanctification as we are of salvation and justification.

Glorification: One day each believer will stand before God and enjoy His presence forever. At that time, finally, what we are and how He sees us will be one and the same. That is glorification, and it comes by grace.

Salvation, justification, sanctification, and *glorification* are all theological terms that describe the process of accepting Christ and becoming like Him. We need God's grace for each part of the process, from the beginning to the end. Grace motivates us to obey Him. Grace shows us our need and offers His solution; it calls us into service. Grace sustains us. The hymn says it well: "Tis grace hath brought me safe thus far, And grace will lead me home."[2]

I heard a beautiful example of the lengths to which God will go to bring us to Himself. In 1995, CoMission missionaries stationed in Stavropol, Russia, were having trouble getting Bibles shipped to them. They learned that somewhere in the city was a warehouse full of Bibles that had been confiscated during the height of Stalin's regime.

The team gathered for prayer. Would God give them grace in the sight of the officials? They could use those long-stored Bibles for the furthering of the kingdom. With fear and trembling, they made their request to the local officials—and permission was granted to remove the Bibles for distribution among the residents of Stavropol.

The following day the CoMission team members hired several Russians and entered the warehouse, planning to load the Bibles onto a truck. One of the hired helpers was a young collegian who had turned his back on God, claiming to be an agnostic. His sullen attitude concerned the team, but they knew he needed the work. It wasn't too big a surprise when they discovered that the young man had disappeared. One of the missionaries went looking for him. He found the young Russian in a remote section of the warehouse, crying.

In spite of his loudly stated beliefs that God did not exist, the young man had hoped to take a Bible for himself and see what it said. The name written on the flyleaf of the first Bible he picked up riveted him to the spot. The name, carefully handwritten years earlier, was that of his grandmother! Out of the thousands of Bibles scattered all over, he had picked up the only one belonging to his grandmother. She had been a godly woman who was persecuted for her faith most of her life.

The young man recognized that there was no coincidence in his choice of Bibles. It was the beginning of his awakening to the things of God. Yahweh-Jireh provided so that grandson could have an encounter with Himself, one that was undeniable. Even his antagonistic heart had to acknowledge the miraculous hand of God in his choosing the one Bible out of thousands that belonged to his grandmother![3] Such is the nature of God's grace.

Not only does God provide us with the grace to bring us to Himself and become like Him, He also provides us with daily grace.

Daily Grace Can't Be Gathered and Stored

We are told in 2 Corinthians 9:8 that He gives "all grace." The mental image that I have of God's provision of all grace is the widow's oil jars in 2 Kings 4:1-7. She had come to the end of her supply. God's servant Elisha instructed her to keep pouring, so she kept on pouring when it looked like there was none to spare.

The oil did not run out until she had filled every jar, jug, and glass available and had no more need of it! Have you ever felt like that? Have you thought that you were running dry? God's grace is like the widow's jar: if you keep pouring, it will not run out. Yet believers often live as though there is not enough of God's grace to go around. We fear for tomorrow.

We need to remember that Yahweh-Jireh's provision is for *today;* it is not something that can be stored up. We see this in the provision of manna when the Israelites were wandering in the desert. Each day they had to go out and collect it. The Israelites were instructed to gather only the amount that they needed—no more and no less. On the sixth day of the week, however, they were allowed to gather enough for the next day, the day God had instructed them to rest. Manna was God's daily provision. However, some of the Israelites decided to gather enough manna for two days. (As the coauthor of *Once-A-Month Cooking,* I can see myself doing the same!) But when they went to eat it the next morning, "it was full of maggots and began to smell" (Exodus 16:20).

Like the Israelites, if we could gather mounds of grace for future troubles, we would. But grace cannot be gathered and stored. It must be accessed on a daily basis. If we are to live by God's grace, we must choose to trust that He is the God who will provide for us *today*. Jesus educated His disciples in that principle when He taught them to pray, "Give us this day, our *daily* bread."

John Blanchard said it well:

> So God supplies perfectly measured grace to meet the needs of the godly. For Daily need—daily grace, Sudden need—sudden grace, Overwhelming need—overwhelming grace.
>
> God's grace is given wonderfully but not wastefully, freely but not foolishly, bountifully but not blindly.[4]

Many women come to me carrying awful burdens. I ask them, "Can you bear today?" Usually they respond, "I can handle today; I just can't stand the thought of tomorrow." Then I ask, "Can you believe that God has given you what you need today? Can you believe that God, Yahweh-Jireh, is looking over time and promises to be there in your future? He will be all you need and more; all you have to do is go to Him for it."

My beautiful friend Jan could not bear the thought of life alone when her marriage broke up. One day, she claimed Isaiah 54:5 for all her tomorrows: "For your Maker is your husband—the LORD Almighty is his name—the Holy One of Israel is your Redeemer; he is called the God of all the earth." Here, in her own words, Jan tells us how Yahweh-Jireh has met her.

> Sometimes, most especially in emotional moments, I say to God, "I am so lonely; would You comfort me and put Your arms around me? I know You are here, but please give me the sense of Your presence that I need just now." I often have a feeling of soft, loving comfort and peace that is difficult to describe, but it is there. Other times God reaches me through friends and family in a way so sudden and precise that it is no coincidence. The phone will ring or a letter will arrive or some other sort of personal contact will be made that is just what I am needing and asking for.
>
> The other amazing thing that happens is that sometimes I have a need that is met in God-like fashion even before I've asked! God sees my emotions and needs and supplies. I lean on this many times through the day as a woman would lean on her mate for that kind of support and fellowship. I would love for God to supply a partner just perfect for me but, in the meantime, He has shown that He can be everything to me at all times. I take great comfort in that and it keeps me content in a

situation that I would like to be different. I trust
God to know and supply in His own special timing.

Tangible and Material

Yahweh-Jireh not only provides for the work in our hearts and gives
us grace for the day, but also He often provides for us in tangible
ways:

- Rosa steeled herself for the bus driver's rage. She had
  pulled herself up the steps of the bus, conscious of the fact
  that she had not a cent to pay her fare. But she couldn't
  walk another step. "O God," she prayed, "provide for
  Your child." As her foot hit the top step, she looked down
  and saw, lying on the floor of the bus, the exact number
  of coins she needed to pay her way home. Quickly she
  scooped up the money and paid her fare with a heart full of
  thanksgiving to her heavenly Father.
- Shelly needed a sweat suit. She felt embarrassed to ask God
  for one because, after all, she had enough clothes. But she
  decided to tell Him what she needed. "Lord, I have many
  nice things, thanks to Your provision, but I think I need a
  sweat suit. If You think I need one, would you provide it?"
  Shelly left her request before the Lord; in fact, she nearly
  forgot about it. One day, the phone rang. A friend who had
  come to visit was calling to say her good-byes before flying
  out in the morning. "By the way, I've left something in a bag
  at the hotel desk, I just couldn't fit it in," she told her. When
  Shelly went to pick up the bag, she was amazed to find the
  exact sweat suit she had imagined when she'd asked God
  for one! It was even the right color! It goes without saying
  that the suit fit. God wouldn't provide for all but one detail.
  When God does it, He does it right!

Does this mean that all we have to do is pray and God will give us what we ask? No. God doesn't always give what is asked for; but He *always* gives what is needed. We see this in 1 Kings 19 after Elijah has run from Jezebel. He was exhausted and had every reason to be. He had challenged Queen Jezebel and her priests and their worship of the pagan gods. After that, he ran what amounted to a marathon. No wonder he was tired! He finally collapsed under a tree and asked God to take his life. Instead of answering his prayer, God gave him sleep. Then God woke him with food and drink, and he slept again. A second time God fed him. God tangibly provided what Elijah needed, not what he'd asked for!

How about you? How has God provided for you? He wants to meet your needs. Blind Bartimaeus heard that Jesus of Nazareth was coming. He knew that this was the man who had healed many people. Maybe He would do something for him. Bartimaeus shouted to get Jesus' attention. People in the crowd shushed him. But he shouted louder. Jesus called to him. In Bartimaeus's excitement, he threw aside his coat and rushed to Jesus. Then Jesus did a strange thing. There was no doubt that the man before Him was blind. Nevertheless Jesus asked him, "What do you want me to do for you?" (Mark 10:51). "Rabbi, I want to see," responded Bartimaeus. When Bartimaeus told Jesus what he wanted Him to do, He did it! Bartimaeus immediately received his sight.

Today, Jesus asks you, "What do you want Me to do for you?" Have you told Him? He changed Blind Bartimaeus into Seeing Bartimaeus, a man who dared to ask and radically experienced the provision of God. He wants to do the same for you.

Plugging the Holes

I knew all the facts about grace. I knew that God is Yahweh-Jireh, the Lord who provides. But those facts didn't seem to affect the core of my being. The godly people around me seemed to be deeply affected by the truth of God's provision, so why wasn't

I? In the book of Deuteronomy, God's children were repeatedly called to "remember." They were to remember where they had come from, what God had given them, and what He had done for them. I felt that God was also calling me to remember. He wanted me to remember all that He had done for me. But how could I remember if I hadn't even *noticed?*

I went back to the image of my life being like a gift box. Although I was learning to see each day as a new gift from God, my box was really more like a sieve. I was allowing God's provision to flow through my life and my day without even stopping to take notice. If I notice and remember what God has done, I will see the pattern of God's work in my life. I decided that I would focus on what is known as "common grace." Common grace is what we experience in the normal things of life. When I chose to dwell on the normal, daily things that God provided for my family and me, I began also to appreciate His generous hand in spiritual areas of my life.

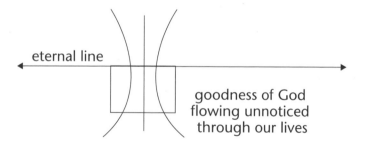

Daily Focusing on God's Provision

Philippians 2:12 says to "continue to work out your salvation." For me, working out my salvation means taking the truths of God and making them mine on a daily basis. What are some habits that you can develop to aid you in making the truths we've studied in this chapter yours?

HOLY HABIT:
Ask God to teach you what His gifts to you are each day.

When I open my gift of today, I intentionally notice that I have been given a good, comfortable bed and clean sheets. The carpet to step onto and the bathroom with hot and cold water are all normal things that God provides. We can cultivate an awareness of His gifts by asking Him to show them to us.

HOLY HABIT:
Thank Him every day.

- For common grace: breathing deeply, seeing color, having a hand with five individually-functioning fingers, being able to swallow without pain
- For temporal provision: shoes, a warm coat, and glasses to wear when you're fifty and your arms aren't long enough to stretch to the point where you can read the fine print
- For special grace in salvation
- For special grace needed to become godly

HOLY HABIT:
Remind yourself that God's grace never runs out.

During a particularly difficult time in her life, Janet decided she needed a reminder that God's grace never runs out. She placed a beautiful blue bottle full of liquid in a visible spot. Whenever she came up against a hard situation (which was almost daily for a long period of time), she would ask God, "Is there enough grace for this?" She mentally took the bottle of God's grace and poured it on the situation. After she had poured out God's grace, she would note that the blue bottle was still full, maybe even fuller than when she started pouring. Then she would say, "Thank you God, that for this, too, there is enough."

HOLY HABIT:
Tell God what you need.

Pray about your needs. There is nothing too trivial to talk to God about. If it's important to you, it's important to Him. At particularly needy times in my life, I have taken a whole sheet in my notebook and titled it, "What do you want Me to do for you?" Then I write down the longings of my heart as a prayer before God. Over it all, I write, "Not my will, but Yours be done." Our God, Yahweh-Jireh, wants you to share your heart's desire with Him.

Take this to heart: God is the Lord who provides. He has provided for your spiritual well-being: you can freely enter into God's presence no matter what the circumstances. His provision is abundant for the need of the moment. He provides for you practically: you can ask Him to meet your financial needs, your soul's longings, whatever lies within your heart. God provided what Elijah needed and not what he asked for. The same is true for us. When we ask, we must recognize that we can trust that He will send what we need. God knows best what to provide.

❋

DO YOU SEE GOD'S PROVISION IN YOUR LIFE? ASK HIM TO TUNE YOUR heart to His provision. He is working. When you are alive to Yahweh-Jireh's residence in you, each day is filled with assurance and confidence. He, Himself, will provide for you, for every aspect of your life, moment by moment.

PRAYER

My Great Provider, as You show me more
and more of Your provisions, forgive me
for accepting the gift without looking up into
Your dear face and thanking You.
Teach me to view each gift as a way to learn
something of Your character. I need Your help.
For, Father, when I begin to understand,
my heart bows low in the face of such generosity.
I am Your child.
Amen.

Study and Discussion Questions

1. Ephesians 1:18-20 refers to the "riches of the glory" that God provides to those that believe (NASB). What does the passage say is the "surpassing greatness of His power" (verse 19)? What does that mean to you?

2. "Gratitude consists in a watchful, minute attention to the particulars of our state, and to the multitude of God's gifts, taken one by one."[5] Read Deuteronomy 26:11 and 1 Thessalonians 5:16-18 and describe how you think you can make this concept a reality in your life today.

3. Read the story of Abraham and Isaac in Genesis 22:1-14, and then read John 1:29. How is the lamb in Genesis 22 like Jesus in John 1?

4. Psalm 145:16 says that God opens His hand and "satisfies the desires of every living thing." Why are we satisfied?

5. Read 1 Timothy 6:17. What are the things in your life that give you security? What does your culture say will give you security? What has God given to you simply for your enjoyment?

6. What do 1 Timothy 6:17 and Philippians 4:19 teach us about God's provision? Why would God bother to provide for us?

7. Study Romans 1:3-5 and make a note of where grace comes from. What is the purpose for grace? Why is grace a provision of God?

8. Read Titus 2:11-14 and make a note of where salvation, justification, and sanctification come from, and how grace is connected with them. Draw a circle on your page, starting with salvation, and write down the provision that God provides to bring us into glorification.

9. What do Psalm 31:15, 74:16, 118:24, and 1 Chronicles 29:14 tell us about each day of our lives? Write your own expression of the truth of these passages.

10. Where have you seen God's provision for you in your life? Share an example of that provision, whether physical, spiritual, or practical.

CHAPTER FIVE

Practicing the Presence of-God

Yahweh-Shammah

BEAUTIFUL INDIAN GIRL APPEARED AT THE MISSION STATION one day. "She looked like a bird from the woods in her colors and jewels, but her eyes were large and soft and gentle, more like a fawn's than a bird's."[1] Mimosa was a young girl who visited missionary Amy Carmichael in Dohnavour, India. While she was there, Mimosa learned two things that she had never known before. She learned that there was a loving God called "Father" and that He made all things. She took those truths to heart and walked back to her village. Mimosa had chosen to make this God her Father. She knew that meant she would have to make changes.

Upon her return to the village she refused to allow the ashes of her ancestral god, Siva, to be placed on her forehead. This and other choices she made to be loyal to her Father infuriated the others in the village. She was beaten repeatedly for her defiance. It was twenty-two years before Mimosa was able to see Amy Carmichael again.

During the intervening years, God had taught Mimosa many things about Himself. Amy Carmichael writes:

> Mimosa stood alone among her people, a woman
> charmed by a beauty she could not show to them. . . .
> Round her were the blazing streets, the little hot houses,
> the curious, unsympathetic faces. . . . But always it was
> as if One only just out of sight were moving through
> the streets with her. What He did with her was good.
> Was He not All-powerful, so that He could direct every-
> thing? Had He not shown her a thousand secret signs
> that she was loved?[2]

I read the story of Mimosa when I was in high school and I identified with her experience. I, too, was alone. My parents had sent me from Africa to boarding school in the United States. I went years without seeing them. It took a year for my letters to reach them and for a return response. My need for intimacy was great. I experienced the comfort of the presence of my heavenly Father in those days.

But as the years passed, my life became full. My home was never quiet. The needs of a busy husband, three small children, and a never-ending stream of guests fractured my time. The sense of God's daily presence became a pleasant memory.

When I turned thirty-two, I realized that God's presence had not been simply a cure for my loneliness during those board-ing school days, but a reality. I wanted to regain a sense of His presence. If I was going to seek to know God, then I needed His moment-by-moment presence so I could spend time with Him, talking, listening, and getting to know His perspective on every aspect of my life.

The Promise of His Presence

God promised His presence to Israel in Ezekiel 48:35: "And the name of the city from that time on will be: [Yahweh-Shammah]

THE LORD IS THERE!" When God made this promise, Israel was in the middle of some of its darkest days. They were in a long exile — far from Jerusalem, the temple, and the land they knew as home. The remnant of Jews in Jerusalem was living in wanton disregard of God. "They were proud of their beautiful jewelry and used it to make their detestable idols and vile images" (Ezekiel 7:20). Things were so bad that "the glory of the LORD departed from over the threshold of the temple . . ." (Ezekiel 10:18). The actual presence of God left the temple because He could not tolerate what was going on in His sanctuary. When His glory left, God left the temple and Jerusalem. Ezekiel 11:23-24 tells us that, "The glory of the LORD went up from within the city and stopped above the mountain east of it." To me, apart from the agony of Christ's death, this is one of the saddest passages in all of Scripture.

The temple and God's presence in it were a crucial part of Israel's national identity. The temple was God's residence. Once the glory of the Lord was gone, gloom and emptiness settled over every Jew. God's absence was a heavy burden. Between Ezekiel chapter ten and the promise of chapter forty-eight there was a deep sense of desolation. Ezekiel's prophecies grew darker. "But as for those whose hearts are devoted to their vile images and detestable idols, I will bring down on their own heads what they have done, declares the Sovereign LORD" (Ezekiel 11:21).

He described what their behavior had been: "But you trusted in your beauty and used your fame to become a prostitute . . . you made for yourself male idols and engaged in prostitution with them . . . and you took your sons and daughters whom you bore to me and sacrificed them as food to the idols" (Ezekiel 16:15-20).

Ezekiel used God's words to tell the rebellious people what would happen to them:

> I will bring you into the desert of the nations and there, face to face, I will execute judgment upon you. (Ezekiel 20:35)

> I will purge you of those who revolt and rebel against
> me. Although I will bring them out of the land where
> they are living, yet they will not enter the land of Israel.
> Then you will know that I am the Lord. (Ezekiel 20:38)

Who were they as a nation without God's presence? What made them unique among all other nations was that they were God's children. He lived with them. Without Him, without their land, who were they?

When God introduced the name Yahweh-Shammah—thereby promising His presence—hope was rekindled for the Jewish nation. After the emptiness they endured, what joy it was for God to say that He is "THE LORD IS THERE"! Hope was renewed because of the promise of the presence of God Himself. God, in the midst of one of the darkest times of Israel's history, affirmed to His people that He would be with them.

God's Presence in Individuals

Probably the most glorious evidence of God's presence was His filling of the tabernacle. It was a portable temple that the Israelites had built according to God's instructions. They called it the Tent of Meeting. When Moses and the people finished the work on the tabernacle, the cloud moved to cover it and the Lord's glory filled the place. The tent was so full of God's glory that even Moses could not enter. God dwelt with His people in the Tent of Meeting.

The portable temple underlined God's desire to live with men, but it wasn't until Jesus came that God's residence in individuals became an option. In John 1:14 it says that the "Word became flesh and made his dwelling among us." Jesus Christ was the presence of God Himself on the earth.

During His time on earth, Jesus promised His presence. He also expressed His desire to be with His disciples beyond this earth: "And surely I am with you always, to the very end of the age"

(Matthew 28:20). Not only that, but He announced the coming of the Spirit of God who would be the Helper, convict of sin, guide into all truth, and make known the heart of Jesus (John 16:7-15).

The presence of the Holy Spirit within us makes us God's temple. Paul wrote:

- Don't you know that you yourselves are God's temple and that God's Spirit lives in you? (1 Corinthians 3:16)
- Do you not know that your body is a temple of the Holy Spirit, who is in you, whom you have received from God? (1 Corinthians 6:19)

The Holy Spirit resides in us only when we invite Him to do so. In response to our invitation, God's glory comes to us just as it did to the temple.

- Christ in you, the hope of glory. (Colossians 1:27)
- And we, who with unveiled faces all reflect the Lord's glory, are being transformed into his likeness with ever-increasing glory, which comes from the Lord, who is the Spirit. (2 Corinthians 3:18)

At times Christ's glorious presence can be seen in individuals. This was true of Carmen, who had endured a tough life. When I first met her, the hardness of her circumstances was reflected in her face, hair, skin, and posture. When she spoke, her voice had an unmistakable edge. She had her "dukes up" to protect herself both physically and emotionally.

One day she came to my home, broken and defeated. We talked together about letting go of all the pain and asking Christ to come into her life and live within her. That afternoon she laid everything at Jesus' feet. She cried as she asked Jesus to come into her heart. I was unprepared for the change that came about in her. The next time we met, I kept shaking my head! Carmen *looked* different!

The harsh lines on her face were smoothed, her hair had lost its dull, lackluster appearance, and she glowed. She announced to me, "Everyone says I look different. I feel like something is healing inside. My situation hasn't changed a bit, but I know that Jesus is with me and that helps me every day!" The power of the presence of God in her life had filled her with joy.

Here are just a few of the Scriptures in which God promises to be present with His children:

- He knew us before we were formed in our mother's womb. (Psalm 139:13-15)
- He says, "Never will I leave you; never will I forsake you." (Hebrews 13:5)
- He will be with us in trials. (Isaiah 43:2)
- He will strengthen and help us. (Isaiah 41:10)
- He will be with us beyond death. (John 14:3)
- He said He would be with us forever. (Matthew 28:20)

God's promise of His presence is for all that seek Him. Throughout Scripture God clearly and emphatically states that He will be with His people. Even in the Old Testament, God sometimes promised His presence to individuals.

God told Jacob: "I am with you and will watch over you wherever you go, and I will bring you back to this land. I will not leave you until I have done what I have promised you" (Genesis 28:15). God made this promise to Jacob even after he had lied and cheated his way into stealing his father's blessing—a blessing that was meant for his older brother Esau. Jacob had feared for his life and ran away to escape his brother's wrath. He was forced to leave all that was dear, including the comfort of his parents' home. Jacob spent his first night in exile alone under the stars. He had a stone for a pillow, a major contrast from the luxuries of his father's dwellings.

While he was sleeping, God spoke to him in a dream, promising to give Jacob and his descendants the land on which Jacob was lying and also promising His presence. Jacob awoke a different man. He was the one who had cheated his brother out of his expected blessing. He had schemed and connived to put himself in place of his brother in his father's affections. He deceived his ancient, blind father, not just by his words, but even to the point of making himself look and smell like his outdoorsy brother. He was a cheat to the core. But in his dream, he was touched by God's promise and he recognized that God was there. He said, "How awesome is this place! This is none other than the house of God; this is the gate of heaven" (Genesis 28:17). Not only that, but selfish Jacob, who wanted everything for himself, even vowed to give back to God ten percent of all of his income. For Jacob, that was radical!

A. W. Tozer wrote that this "loving Personality dominates the Bible, walking among the trees of the garden and breathing fragrance over every scene. Always a living Person is present, speaking, pleading, loving, working, and manifesting Himself whenever and wherever His people have the receptivity necessary to receive the manifestation."[3] We need to seek to have this understanding of Jesus' vital presence in every aspect of our life. A passionate relationship with an ever-present Savior changes a person forever.

God's Presence Gives Strength

When we experience God's presence, we are strengthened to face the difficulties and trials life holds for us. That point was brought home to me through the testimony of a Chinese pastor who spoke at the Conference on Evangelism in the Philippines a number of years ago. In a trembling voice, he told how he had been imprisoned for his faith. His solitary confinement was oppressive, and guards hovered near so he could not pray or sing aloud. His heart longed to have the freedom to speak and sing openly with his heavenly Father. He begged God to allow him to have the joy of worship out loud. Even to him, the request seemed outrageous. How could he ever be free of the guards?

One day the door to his cell swung open and a guard shoved him roughly out into the light. He was told he'd been given a job. They marched the pastor out to the corner of the prison grounds. As he and his armed guard neared the prison wall, an overwhelming stench assaulted their nostrils. He realized that he was being sent to clean out the sewer!

The heat of the sun made the rank fumes all the more intense. He wondered how he could manage to work under those circumstances. A few feet from the pit, the soldier, with his nose pinched firmly between two fingers, threw a shovel at the pastor. "I'll be back in a few hours to check your progress," he said. Slowly the man lowered himself into the filthy muck, bowed by the enormity of the disgusting task he'd been given. Then he realized that he was alone! No human being could stand to be within smelling distance; therefore no one was within hearing distance either. With dawning understanding he lifted his head and began to sing, "I come to the garden alone. . . ." The pastor told the audience that the stinking, filthy sewer was turned into a garden by the very presence of God during his worship.

What sewer are you facing in your life? Is the smell of loneliness overwhelming? Are you disgusted by your circumstances? Or is your life so busy that you just don't have time to recognize that God is there? His name is "THE LORD IS THERE." Mark this down: God is with you. His presence can give you the strength to face any circumstance.

God's residence within Paul made him able to face even the most incredible difficulties with head held high. He said that he'd been

> . . . beaten up more times than I can count, and at death's door time after time. I've been flogged five times with the Jews' thirty-nine lashes, beaten by Roman rods three times, pummeled with rocks once. I've been shipwrecked three times, and immersed in the open sea for a night and a day. In hard traveling year in and year out, I've had to ford rivers, fend off

robbers, struggle with friends, struggle with foes. I've been at risk in the city, at risk in the country, endangered by desert sun and sea storm, and betrayed by those I thought were my brothers. I've known drudgery and hard labor, many a long and lonely night without sleep, many a missed meal, blasted by the cold, naked to the weather. (2 Corinthians 11:23-27, MSG)

In light of all his troubles, Paul's statement in Philippians 4:13 is more powerful still: "I can do everything through him who gives me strength."

Paul's consciousness of God's presence was so strong that he said, "For in him we live and move and have our being" (Acts 17:28). In other words, he lived with an active awareness that God's presence enveloped him and everything he did.

The understanding of God's all-encompassing presence was a reality to Paul in a way that many of us cannot grasp. Traditionally, Christians have thought of God and heaven as "out there." God seems distant and removed from that which pertains to us. But during Paul's day there was a different understanding of where God and heaven were. Theologian Dallas Willard says,

A totally good and competent God is right here with us to look after us. And His presence is precisely what the word heaven . . . conveys in the biblical record. . . . Nothing—no human being or institution, no time, no space, no spiritual being, no event—stands between God and those who trust him. The "heavens" are always there with you no matter what, and the "first heaven," in biblical terms, is precisely the atmosphere or air that surrounds your body.[4]

All that God is envelops us. Everything that we need for the well-being of our souls encompasses us.

But I Don't Sense God's Presence with Me!

But what about the times that we don't see God's presence? Does that mean He isn't there? Of course not. We are told over and over in Scripture that He is with us. Hebrews 11:1 tells us that faith is believing what we can't see. Just because we can't see God doesn't mean He's not there. In order to bolster our faith, God has at times given us a "window" that allows us to see the supernatural, invisible world. In 2 Kings the prophet Elisha's servant woke up one morning to discover that the Arabian army had surrounded their city. He was paralyzed with fear and cried out to Elisha, "Oh, my lord, what shall we do?" (6:15).

Elisha told the servant they had no need to fear because "those who are with us are more than those who are with them" (6:16), and then he prayed and asked God to open the servant's eyes. God answered Elisha's prayer, and the servant was able to see what had been invisible to him before: the hills were full of horses and chariots of fire, surrounding and protecting Elisha. God's presence was overpowering! We can imagine how that servant's fear was changed to gladness.

Cultivating an Awareness of God's Presence

Once we invite Christ to be a part of our lives, how do we live in active awareness of that fact?

HOLY HABIT:

SILENCE YOUR HEART DAILY SO THAT YOU CAN BE SENSITIVE TO GOD'S-PRESENCE.

George Butterick said, "Prayer is listening as well as speaking, receiving as well as asking. . . . And in the deepest mood is friendship held in reverence."[5] Just as there are no uncomfortable silences between good friends, we can sit in meaningful silence with God. Silence is a part of prayer just as it is a part of earthly friendships. Unless we "have ears to hear," how can we hear His voice or sense His presence?

You might be a frantic mother with young children, an executive trying to keep home and work together, or simply a person exhausted beyond words. God is present with you; He hears your thoughts and understands that at times your communion with Him comes out of the workings of your body. His presence makes ordinary things sacred.

Do you want to know more of God's presence in your life? Take time to "be still, and know that I am God" (Psalm 46:10). Many of us get too caught up in the rush and busyness of life—no wonder we don't sense God's presence!

My friend Agnes is a news addict. She likes to know everything that is going on in the world. Agnes also loves God with her whole heart. She told me that she has to discipline herself not to turn on the television or radio every time she has a free moment. She finds that the noise and loud voices crowd out her ability to concentrate on anything else, and in the midst of that it is hard to hear God's voice.

Several years ago, she made the choice to limit the time she listens to news and current events programs, so she can be still and experience God's residence in her life. She learned to quiet the demanding voices of other things in order to maintain a consciousness of God's indwelling presence. When she did, Agnes found that communion with her heavenly Father deepened and intensified. She was no longer distracted.

HOLY HABIT:
Ask God to help you see life through His eyes.

Recently we watched a golf tournament on television. The commentator mentioned the major improvement one player was enjoying in his putting. Apparently during the off season, the player had gone to his eye doctor and discovered that his glasses were the wrong prescription. With a simple change of lenses, his entire view changed and his golf game radically improved! Because of his new perspective, he was in contention for the championship.

For many years I went through life just like the golfer. I could hardly see what God was trying to show me. But once I began to understand that He dwells within me, I asked Him to let me see things in my life through His eyes. It was as if I took off an old pair of glasses with the wrong prescription and put on a new pair with the correct one. Everything looked different!

As God changed the "lenses" through which I viewed my life, I saw that all around me were gifts from God that I had not recognized before. He showed me that many of the things I had taken for granted were from Him. Many of them were simple things but, for the first time, I saw them for what they were—gifts from His hand. Whenever I receive a gift, I can hear my mother's voice, "When you accept a gift, look up into the face of the giver and say 'thank you.'" I learned to thank God for the wonderful feeling of being able to slip into a bathtub of warm water, a cozy bed, the sweetness of a spring morning, and so on. This exercise was the cultivation of awareness of the presence of God in my life. After years of looking up to the Giver of all things in my life, I found that I wanted to please Him more than anything else. I found I was saying, "If it would please You" many times a day. It was my way of saying, "Your will be done." As we develop a consciousness of His presence and ask Him to give us His perspective, the way we see things and events in our lives will change.

HOLY HABIT:
Talk to God throughout the day.

The psalmist David wrote, "On my bed I remember you; I think of you through the watches of the night" (Psalm 63:6). God was real to him at all hours of the day or night. We, too, can commune with God throughout the day. When we do, we grow more aware of His presence in our lives.

Paul tells us to pray continually (1 Thessalonians 5:17). At first glance this may seem impossible, but because God lives where our thoughts are born, we can train our minds to address all our thoughts as prayers to Him. He knows our thoughts anyway. James Borst was referring to this when he said, "[God] is closer to my true self than I am myself."[6]

I have a mental image of how this works. When I waken in the morning, I open the door of my mind and there God is. He lives right there, in the part of me that thinks. God has put His Spirit into the part of me that is who I really am.

When I go to the grocery store, my thoughts can be my own, or I can invite Him to participate with me. When I reach the apples and need to decide what kind and how many to get, I think—just as if I was conversing with a friend—*How many should I get, Lord? Would the Golden Delicious be best?* I choose to pass all my thinking through the filter of His presence. When it comes time to prepare dinner, I address my thoughts to Him as I cook. When I am in a discussion with a friend, rather than wondering to myself, *How can I best respond to this?* I ask God that question. Sometimes I talk to Him out loud when I'm driving. Rather than wishing for a parking spot, I talk to God about it. That, to me, is what Paul meant by praying continually.

❋

WHEN OUR HEARTS ARE CAPTURED BY THE TRUTH OF GOD'S PRESENCE IN every moment, in every space that surrounds us, they will naturally overflow in response. God, who is as close as the air we breathe, holds both the past and the future in eternity! We are free to fill every moment with His presence because He is in control! We can relish each moment with God in abandonment. When you acknowledge His presence in your life you will discover, as Moses did, that His presence is necessary for survival. He will do revolutionary things like He did for the Chinese pastor. He will be with you in practical ways, providing and protecting. His presence teaches you His perspective. As you walk with Him daily, His character becomes a part of yours.

The final fulfillment of God's promise to live with His people is found in the last book of the Bible where God reaffirms that His all-time plan for humankind is to dwell with Him. "And I heard a loud voice from the throne saying, 'Now the dwelling of God is with men, and he will live with them. They will be his people, and God himself will be with them and be their God. He will wipe every tear from their eyes'" (Revelation 21:3-4). What we now know of God's presence is nothing compared to what it will be. When we are finished with life on this earth, we will enjoy the presence of God without interruption. Nothing will keep us from clearly reflecting His image.

PRAYER

Increase my awareness, O Lord, of this
great gift You have given me.
May each day take on new meaning
as I understand Your presence in it.
Cultivate in me a sensitivity to
Your residence and all that it implies.
May the reflection of Your character in me
become clearer to the world as I grasp who You are.
In the Great Name of my God,
Amen.

Study and Discussion Questions

1. In Ezekiel 10:18-19 and Ezekiel 11:22-24 we read about the presence of God departing the temple. What would your life be like without the presence of God?

2. We have said that God's presence is practical. According to Exodus 33:14 and Matthew 11:29, what is one practical benefit of God's presence? How can God's presence do that in your life?

3. God said, "Just as I have been with Moses, I will be with you, I will not fail you nor forsake you" (Joshua 1:5). Rewrite this verse to personalize it for yourself and those you love. Then read on through verse 9 and make a note of those things that can be appropriated for your life.

4. Read Psalm 4:6, 44:3, and 89:15. What is the common thread in all three verses? How do you think God's presence provides that for you in your daily life?

5. Psalm 16:7-11 mentions other results of God's presence. What are they? How have you experienced these in your life?

6. Write a prayer to God asking Him to open your eyes to the gifts He has given you, and thank Him for the ones of which you are aware.

7. According to Matthew 28:20, how long are the saints ensured of the presence of God before they go to heaven?

8. The Chinese pastor experienced God's presence in the prison cesspool. Explain how the promises of Deuteronomy 31:6, Psalm 91:9-10, and Isaiah 43:2 could be made a reality in your life just as they were in the pastor's life.

9. What does the promise found in Matthew 18:20 mean for a group of believers who meet together? If we would live as if we believe that, how would it change the nature of our meetings with God's people?

10. How can we live today in active awareness of His presence? Give an example of that from your own life.

CHAPTER SIX

Healing Wounded Hearts

Yahweh-Rophe

HEN I FIRST MET BETSY, I COULD TELL THAT THERE WAS more to her than met the eye, and I wanted to get to know her better. One day as we sat in the afternoon sun, she told me her story: "My mother, a Native American, worked as a maid on a large plantation in Virginia. When she was fifteen, she became pregnant—the plantation owner's son was the father—and she was banished to a small, isolated cabin, far from the main house. My mother died shortly after I was born."

Although Betsy was reared in the big house, she never received a hug or kiss from anyone in the family. She was an unwanted burden, and she knew it. "I felt rejected and confused. I tried so hard to be good so that they would love me, but no matter what I did, nothing worked," Betsy told me. Just as she was about to learn how to read, Betsy was told she had to earn her keep and could no longer attend school.

She worked hard, but the family continued to treat her with disdain and rejection. When she turned eleven, she could stand it no longer. She left on the train and never looked back. "I was all alone in the world, with no one I could trust," Betsy said. "I was afraid of being caught by a truant officer so I worked in hotels in the evenings, and during the day I hid in a boarding room closet. I didn't get much sleep, but it was better than being sent back to the plantation."

As soon as she could save enough money, Betsy purchased an insurance policy, providing her with the assurance of a burial plot. More than anything, she feared being buried in an unmarked, public grave.

One Sunday she was taken to church. It was her first introduction to a loving God. The Sunday school teacher told the class that God could see who they really were and that He loved them. The teacher's words pierced Betsy's heart, but she moved to another town before she learned more about God. Still, she never forgot the message.

Betsy's young heart broke from all the early rejection and she began her adult life longing for love. But throughout her life, at different times, God called out to her until finally at age sixty, she decided to teach herself to read so she could read the Bible and learn about God. She said, "As I studied Scripture and got to know God, His love began to fill the holes in my heart. For the first time in my life, I felt I belonged. Someone loved me!"

When I met Betsy she was ninety-seven years old. Laid at the feet of Yahweh-Rophe, the God who heals, the deep wounds of her unloving past no longer burdened her. In her twilight years, Betsy had discovered her identity as a child of the Healer King. Today she glows with a radiance that can come only from having experienced firsthand the healing touch of the love of God.

Bitter Waters Made Sweet

God introduced Himself as the God who heals when the Israelites desperately needed a touch from Him. After four hundred years of slavery in Egypt, God had led them into freedom. He had miraculously delivered them from their enemies and from the waves of the Red Sea. They must have had a sense of invincibility as they marched across the desert with their backs to Egypt and their faces toward the Promised Land. They were on a roll.

Every time I read about the Israelites' experience in the desert, I'm reminded of the intense heat of the tropical sun. When I lived in Africa, we did not dare put a thermometer in the sun because it would zoom past 120 degrees and explode. We only measured the temperature in the relative protection of the shade of a large tree.

When I was a child, I thought there could be no place on earth hotter than the Ituri forest during the dry season, until we flew to Khartoum, Sudan. As we stepped off the plane onto the tarmac, we were blasted with furnace-like heat. It was so hot no one spoke. As we trudged toward an even hotter terminal, we remembered reading that ancient rulers would not spend summer in the desert because it was so hot that a lizard could fry attempting to cross a plaza. I believed it, because we felt like we were going to cook!

The Israelites crossed a desert much like the one we visited in Sudan. The heat must have been unrelenting. Exodus 15 tells us they traveled for three days without finding any water. Children were crying and the adults' faces were set in grim apprehension of death on the sand. Finally, an oasis came into sight. The people rejoiced and rushed forward to drink, but the first to get a taste shouted in warning, "*Marah!*" Bitter! All the victories of the previous days were forgotten in the huge disappointment. The fear of death was palpable among the travelers.

Angry Israelites accused Moses of leading them to destruction. They told him it would have been better to die as slaves in Egypt than to perish for lack of water in the desert. Moses turned to God in his desperation to meet the thirst of thousands of people. God directed him to a piece of wood, and told him what to do with it. Moses threw the wood into the water and it became sweet. "There the LORD made a decree and a law for them, and there he tested them. He said, 'If you listen carefully to the voice of the LORD your God and do what is right in his eyes, if you pay attention to his commands and keep all his decrees, I will not bring on you any of the diseases I brought on the Egyptians, for *I am the LORD, who heals you*'" (Exodus 15:25-26, emphasis added).

The wood Moses threw into the water had no power in and of itself, but it foreshadowed God's salvation of His people. First Peter 2:24-25 says, "He himself bore our sins in his body on the tree, so that we might die to sins and live for righteousness; by his wounds you have been healed. For you were like sheep going astray, but now you have returned to the Shepherd and Overseer of your souls." In the New Testament healing came about through the cross of Christ. But Christ's death on the cross provided not only healing for salvation, but also healing from the hurts brought about by sin.

Do You Need Healing from Bitterness?

Is your soul sick? Ellen's was. She was struggling in a pressured marriage. As we talked, she told me how much she wanted to please God. But then she recounted her husband's offenses, one after another. Ellen said she awoke each day so full of resentment that it was nearly impossible to pray. At breakfast, she would go over in her mind all of the past hurts, just in case she had forgotten the details. She thought about her list of grievances all day and added to that list any new ones. Ellen was unhappy and bitter.

I could identify with Ellen. At one point in my life I carried emotional "boxes" of grievances from one day to the next. I spent much of each day reviewing the details of the contents of those boxes. I found that by noon, I had spent so much time going over each offense that I had little time to savor the evidence of the goodness of God in my life. When I finally admitted to myself what was happening, I determined that the old boxes had to go. The process was difficult because the roots of bitterness had penetrated every area of my life. Like cleaning out a closet, I had to clean out my heart and mind, *one thought at a time*. Sometimes the process took weeks other times, years. Some of my bitter feelings were so deep they were hidden from even me; others I was adept at covering up. When I realized this, I asked God to make my heart tender to His leading. As He brought thoughts and feelings to my awareness, I placed each one under the blood of Jesus. In my mind I imagined myself actually handing those thoughts and feelings to Christ with a prayer on my heart, "Lord, put this one under Your blood."

Do you wrestle with carrying offenses and griefs from one day to the next? George MacDonald spoke to this human tendency:

> It has been well said that no man ever sank under the burden of the day. It is when tomorrow's burden is added to the burden of today that the weight is more than a man can bear. Never load yourselves so, my friends. If you find yourselves so loaded, at least remember this: it is your own doing, not God's. He begs you to leave the future to Him, and mind the present.[1]

Are you carrying yesterday's burdens? Do you need healing?

Many people's lives are broken and shattered by past pain and grief, whether from the anguish of a difficult child, the memories of a nightmarish work experience, or a husband's or child's wounds. Others suffer from a childhood abuse or rape—ugly things that have caused tremendous damage. But when we carry our hurts from day to day, our lives are filled with heaviness.

Emotional baggage can even bring with it physical symptoms. Headaches, stomachaches, exhaustion, and many other ailments can come from not dealing with the past. Before he confessed his sins of adultery and murder, David wrote, "My wounds fester and are loathsome because of my sinful folly. I am bowed down and brought very low; all day long I go about mourning. My back is filled with searing pain; there is no health in my body. I am feeble and utterly crushed; I groan in anguish of heart" (Psalm 38:5-8).

Not all illness is due to unresolved emotional baggage, but some of it is. A counselor friend of mine told me about Jeffrey, a middle-aged man who came to see her. He had recently been diagnosed with multiple sclerosis. He was haggard, drawn, and very sick. Besides carrying the terrible burden of a degenerative disease, he was also deeply grieved because his wife had left him and their children for another man. My friend worked with this man until he moved out of the area.

Several years later, the counselor was at a party and was shocked to see Jeffrey. He looked totally different. His once haggard face had filled out; he looked strong and vital. She slipped up next to him to say hello. He turned to her and smiled. "I look a lot different from the last time you saw me, don't I?" he asked. "It took me a long time to take your advice, but I was finally able to forgive my wife for abandoning us. When I forgave her, I began to regain my strength, and now I'm feeling wonderful!" Jeffrey experienced not only spiritual and emotional healing, but physical healing as well, when he was able to forgive and allow Yahweh-Rophe to restore him!

In Matthew 18 we read of the generous king who forgave his servant a massive debt. The debt was so large that he could never have paid it back, even if he had worked all his life. Then in the face of such incredible generosity, the forgiven servant went out and tried to squeeze payment for a small sum he was owed by a fellow servant. When the king learned about it he was "moved with anger [and] handed him over to the torturers until he should repay all that was owed him" (Matthew 18:34, NASB). When we carry around the offenses of the past and do not forgive, we are, just like the servant, handed over to the torturers of our own soul. Bitterness, grief, and pain can only torment our hearts and damage our lives. Unwillingness to forgive is sin.

As Yahweh-Rophe, God's response to all sin is, "'I have seen his ways, but I will heal him; I will guide him and restore comfort to him, creating praise on the lips of the mourners in Israel. Peace, peace, to those far and near,' says the LORD. 'And I will heal them'" (Isaiah 57:18-19).

When Angela came to me for help, she told me her life was miserable and nothing was going right. As she spoke, bitterness toward her ex-husband poured out. When she had talked herself out, I asked her if she wanted to be free of her ex-husband. She replied to me that she already was free because they were no longer married. I replied, "No, Angela, he has as strong of a hold, or stronger, on you now than when you were married." Why? Because her bitterness and lack of forgiveness was hurting *her,* not him. Until she could forgive him, he would continue to have power over her. It took several weeks for Angela to come to the point where she was willing to forgive her ex-husband. When she did, she kept saying that she didn't know what it was like to be free until she forgave.

Right after the Lord's Prayer Jesus says, "For if you forgive men for their transgressions, your heavenly Father will also forgive you. But if you do not forgive men, then your Father will not forgive your transgressions" (Matthew 6:14-15, NASB). Why would Jesus place that kind of condition on us? Because of His great love. He knows that when we hold on to resentment and bitterness, it will consume and destroy us. This is particularly important in our world, where being wronged is such a major issue. Much of our bitterness is caused by the sin and neglect of someone else. The pain of being wronged is like hot lava within our souls. Lack of forgiveness burns a tender heart. That's why Christ wants us to give Him that pain. He wants us to be whole and complete. He asks us to forgive, to release the pain and bitterness to Him. Forgiveness heals our souls and makes our days brand-new again.

Not only does God take our pain when we forgive, but He will also judge the wrong that has been done against us. I find it easy to say with my mouth that God is my avenger, but my heart thinks that He takes a long time to avenge! However, if I am to obey God's Word that tells me to "hate what is evil; cling to what is good" (Romans 12:9), I must yield myself to God who is Yahweh-Rophe and allow Him to take care of the evil done to me.

If you have been betrayed, forgiveness may seem unfair or unjust. And it is! In his book *What's So Amazing About Grace?*, Philip Yancey points out that forgiveness is an unnatural act. If our God was not Yahweh-Rophe, forgiveness would be an impossible burden. But He heals our bitterness, making the way for us to forgive others.

Getting to Forgiveness

Joseph had every right to be bitter. His brothers had sold him into slavery and he had spent the best years of his life serving other people in a land far away from his home. He would have been entitled to every kind of resentment and bitterness because he had been mistreated. But Joseph provides one of the most powerful examples of forgiveness. Joseph said to his brothers, "Don't be afraid. Am I in the place of God? You intended to harm me, but God intended it for good to accomplish what is now being done" (Genesis 50:19-20). This statement reveals how he had been able to forgive his brothers: he had chosen to look at his experience from God's perspective. When our focus is on what has been done *to* us rather than what God has done *for* us, we destroy our lives on an ongoing basis. What was the result of Joseph's offering of forgiveness? Family healing. The family was reunited, brought together and preserved because of his forgiving spirit. Lives were saved because Joseph chose to seek God's perspective and forgive.

But, you ask, how can I forgive when what happened to me was so wrong?

Recognize What Forgiveness Is Not
First and foremost, *forgiveness is not merely an option*. To have a right relationship with God we *have to* forgive (Matthew 6:14-15).

Forgiveness is not forgetting. To forget an event is to ask our minds to behave in a way counter to how God created them. He has given us marvelous memories. I recently heard someone say that forgiveness is handling memories appropriately. It is the freedom that comes when you are reminded of that past pain and it no longer has the power to hurt you. That's what God can provide for us!

Forgiveness is not saying that whatever was done against you is all right. Forgiveness is laying the blood of Jesus Christ over the offense and giving Him the grief and pain. It is letting Him bear the hurt. It is the freedom that comes when we know that we are right with God and He will take care of everything else.

Ask for God's Help to Forgive

When I find forgiveness impossible to extend on my own, the cry of my heart is, "God, forgive through me." With that prayer, I am saying to Him, "I will be the conduit of Your eternal, unlimited forgiveness and I stand on the final act of forgiveness offered on the cross of Your Son."

Betty's husband, Stan, and his partners had worked hard for many years to develop the successful company they owned. When Stan was in his mid-fifties, the partners began to squeeze him out of daily operations. Eventually, they made life so unbearable that he sold his part of the business and got out. Betty was furious. Stan had invested his entire life in that company and those men. They had no right to treat him like that! Within weeks, she found herself desperately unhappy. What had happened?

Betty examined her heart before God and found that rage and unforgiveness were eating her up. Everywhere she turned, there were reminders of how unfairly Stan had been treated. Betty realized that unless she forgave those men, she would never be able to shake the deep unhappiness. She also saw that Stan needed her to be free of resentment so he could begin his own process of healing. Betty fell to her knees and sobbed her heart out to God. The first time she named each of the men and forgave them, it was agony! Then every time Betty was reminded of the injustice done to Stan, she named each man as she prayed out loud. Her prayer was that God would help her as she forgave them. At first, she had to forgive them many times a day. Now, years later, Betty says with a laugh that it was the best thing that happened to them! She and Stan have enjoyed many worry-free years together, and they have learned how to walk in active forgiveness.

Recognize That You Have Been Forgiven

When we realize God has forgiven us of the offenses we have done against Him, we are better disposed to forgive. After all, if we didn't, we would be exactly like the ungrateful servant who was forgiven so much, yet refused to forgive the one who owed him a little. God has forgiven us of everything that we have done. Our sin builds a barrier between us and Him. Once we have asked God to forgive us, the only thing that leaves that barrier there is our unwillingness to forgive those who have offended us. When we look at what God has done for us, our hearts can overflow in a love response to Him by forgiving others.

Not only does God heal our souls from bitterness and sin, He also heals our bodies. He offers both spiritual and physical healing.

All Physical Healing Comes from God

Throughout Jesus' ministry, He healed the blind, the crippled, the lepers, and He even raised people from the dead. Does He perform similar miraculous healings today? I believe that He can and does. Cal has a plaque hanging in his office inscribed with the French words:

> Je le pansai,
> Dieu le guerit.
> (Ambroise Pare, 1510–1590)

It means "I dress the wound, God heals it." The message reminds him that any healing, whether from a bottle or the hand of a doctor, comes from God. Medicine works because of God. He sustains life consistently. Because of the pattern that emerges when one studies the body, the medical world can conclude what a "normal" physical profile looks like. When an aspirin relieves a headache, that is the work of God because of the marvelous predictability of His creation. Any healing, whether "miraculous" or not, comes directly from Him.

Our dear friends, Ericka and Roberto, learned that their eight-year-old son, Jaime, had leukemia. We wondered how this trial would affect their new faith in Christ. We felt frustrated because of the distance between us. They were in Ecuador and we were in Colorado. Cal was also concerned about the medical treatment Jaime would receive. Roberto called to say that they were trusting God to work in Jaime's body and that they had the best doctors available. We received copies of all the tests done and Cal carefully reviewed them with specialists in the United States. Roberto said, "God gave us the doctors and we are counting on them to help us, but God is above them and He's the one really doing the work!" Our friends had a clear understanding that God often uses doctors to do His healing. Today, Jaime is in remission, and both he and his family recognize that God has touched his body.

When our bodies are injured or hurting in some way, we can be distracted from the care of our souls. This is so shortsighted— tragic, really. Why? Because our bodies were created for time to house our souls that were made for eternity. Physical healing is important to us because we live in time, but soul healing is critical for our time *and* eternity. So often we put physical healing over soul healing, but when we understand who God is and how He views time and eternity, we are able to put physical healing in proper perspective and soul keeping takes priority.

Soul-Keeping Habits

As believers, we need daily cleansing, daily healing, from anything that would keep us from walking uprightly before God. We need to practice certain habits in order to keep ourselves spiritually healthy.

HOLY HABIT:
CLEANSE YOUR HEART DAILY.

Not long ago, a friend of mine bought a lovely, expensive house. The previous owners had enjoyed the help of two live-in maids to clean and cook. My friend arrived with the moving van expecting to move into a clean place, but was horrified to discover that it was filthy. In spite of having the help of two maids, the former occupants had allowed piles of dirt to stick and build up in the corners of rooms, and rat droppings were everywhere. The beauty of the home and the furnishings had covered up the grime until they moved out. The dirt and droppings could only have accumulated over time. Regular cleaning would have eliminated that.

Most of us would not allow that dirt to pile up in our house. We would be appalled. But sadly, we are not so careful to clean our hearts, even though they are home to the King of kings. Would you dare have a king come to your residence without turning it upside down and cleaning every nook and cranny? How often do we do heart housekeeping to make it a fit place for the King to dwell?

What is heart housekeeping? It is going to God and asking Him if there is anything that you are carrying that does not please Him. It is asking Him to reveal what has built up that would keep you from a right relationship with Him. We should do it regularly because it shows us things for which we need to seek God's healing.

For me, spiritual housekeeping means making an inventory of what is in my heart. I ask God to show me if I need to forgive someone or if I harbor wrong attitudes that could slip out. I seek to cultivate a sensitivity to Him that will become a habit when I am unable to will myself to do it. For example, I try not to think critical thoughts about people. My prayer has been, "Lord, give me your perspective on that person. Because when I am eighty, I may not be in my right mind and I want there to be a sweetness in me that is a habit beyond my mental control because You have bathed and cleansed me with Your blood."

To put feet to that prayer, I will often look around a waiting room at an airport or doctor's office and choose to sit near someone others might avoid. As I sit there I pray, "Lord, this might be the closest this person comes to the love of God today. Flow through me, even if I do not have a chance to say anything profound. Just let me show her common human kindness to reflect Your love."

HOLY HABIT:

AVOID THOSE THINGS THAT DISTRACT YOU FROM A GOD-CENTERED LIFE.

What are those things that could disrupt a pure walk with God? Believers need to answer that question for themselves. Just as in the medical world different bodies have higher and lower resistances to diseases, so in the spiritual world our levels of resistance to potential distraction or sin vary. For some, a picture on a billboard could trigger thinking that would carry them away from a God-centered thought life. For others, it could be a commercial, a book, language on a television show, a certain kind of movie, or something else. For example, Shelly rarely allows herself to look at catalogs because they stimulate in her a discontent with what she has. But for me, a catalog is pure fun!

When Cal was in medical school, he was on call many nights. I spent a number of those long, lonely evenings absorbed in good romantic novels. However, I noticed that when Cal walked in the door, he didn't meet my expectations! I soon realized that the characters in the books I was reading were wealthy, always rested, and if they were doctors, they never seemed to be up half the night delivering babies. My husband was deeply fatigued and terribly stressed. There was no way he could measure up to the heroes in the books. The unrealistic world of the novels created in me a dissatisfaction with my life. I had to make a choice to stop focusing on the fantasy world of the books I was reading and work with what I had. For me, the books distracted me from working toward the goals I had set out for my life.

HOLY HABIT:

SEEK TO DEMONSTRATE YOUR CHOICE TO FORGIVE THOSE WHO HAVE WRONGED YOU.

When I have been hurt or wronged, I ask God to help me forgive those who are responsible. Then I ask Him to show me something to do that can symbolize my forgiveness. Most of the time, it would only enflame the situation if I did something directly for the person who has hurt me. Instead, God shows me someone else who can represent that hurt and I do something for that person: sometimes it has meant preparing a meal or giving the gift of a sweater, new shoes, or some sweet-smelling lotion. These little tokens are my way of turning from evil to good. I leave one thing behind while I reach for another. This does not deny the hurt and leave my emotions in a vacuum; it allows me to acknowledge them and helps me to focus on returning good for evil. The greatest biblical example of that was Jesus on the cross, when He forgave even though none had asked for His forgiveness.

*

YAHWEH-ROPHE IS THE HEALER OF OUR EMOTIONAL WOUNDS. HE heals the body and the soul from grief, and He shows us when we are wounded and unable to be a clear channel of His Spirit. He is the means by which we can forgive the wrongs done to us. He restores our hearts, souls, and bodies when we look to Him.

P R A Y E R

My God,
Your wholeness is in such contrast to my brokenness.
Pour Yourself into me that I may be filled with Your Holiness.
You are my only hope for complete
healing and perfect restoration.
I need You moment by moment.
Your Needy Child,
Amen.

STUDY AND DISCUSSION QUESTIONS

1. Study the story of Lazarus in John 11:1-45. What are some of the characteristics of God that Jesus displays in this passage?

2. John 11:4,15, and 40 reveal Jesus' purpose in operating from a different time frame. What was His purpose? Was it accomplished? Write down the verses from John 11:1-45 where Jesus refers to a plan bigger than a human one.

3. How can the principles of the story in John 11:1-45 apply to your life? What does this story tell us about how He views us in our sickness and death?

4. What do Romans 5:12 and 1 John 5:17 tell us about sin?

5. What does God say in Isaiah 1:13-20 about sin and what we are to do about it? What does the Lord tell us He will do to our sin, and what is the blessing for obedience?

6. From today's news, give an example of how the world can contaminate us.

7. In Psalm 41:4 David asks God to heal him. Read Isaiah 57:18-19, Jeremiah 3:22, 17:14, 30:17, and Luke 4:18, making notes of what God can do with a request such as David's.

8. God tells us that we must forgive. How often are we to forgive according to Matthew 18:21-22? Why does He tell us to forgive in Mark 11:25? Whose example are we to follow as seen in Ephesians 4:32 and Colossians 3:13? Add any other insights you might have discovered from these verses.

9. What soul keeping do you need to do?

10. According to Hebrews 12:15, the root of bitterness defiles many. How does that happen? Can you think of an example of that truth from your own life or someone else's? Read Ephesians 4:31-32. What does it say we should put in place of bitterness, rage, and anger?

11. How does the fact that God is Healer help you live life intentionally?

CHAPTER SEVEN

Finding Hope Every Day

Yahweh-Nissi

ONLY A FEW WEEKS HAD PASSED SINCE THE ISRAELITES HAD seen God's miracle at Marah. In the ensuing days, He had sent manna and appeared to them in a cloud by day and a pillar of fire by night. But when they came again to a place without water, they forgot all that God had done for them since He had brought them out of Egypt and they cried, "Why did you bring us up out of Egypt to make us and our children and livestock die of thirst?" (Exodus 17:3).

Once again God gave them water, but then came the news: the Amalekites were threatening war. The Amalekites had long been enemies of Israel. Nathan Stone writes of them:

> Moved by suspicion, jealousy, and fear, they resented
> the presence of such a multitude of strange people in
> the wilderness and were determined to prevent their
> passage through it. Thus they opposed the purpose
> and plan. They had first carried on a sort of harassing,

guerilla campaign against Israel. Then apparently they
came out against them in open battle.[1]

Moses was commander-in-chief, and Joshua, as his first lieuten-
ant, was to lead the men into combat. It was customary in those
days for the commander-in-chief to place himself at a vantage
point where he could observe the conflict, send orders, and serve
to encourage his troops. Moses took his staff, the rod of God, and
with Aaron and Hur went up to the top of the hill overlooking
the battle site (Exodus 17:10).

You will remember that the staff had originally been Moses'
shepherd's tool, but it had come to represent God's presence to
the Israelites:

> It was the rod, as the banner of God, which brought
> the glory. . . . This rod was the rod of God, the God-
> given rod, the wonder-working rod, the rod which
> brought the terrible plagues on Egypt, which opened
> a path in the Red Sea. . . . It was the rod of God's
> mighty hand and outstretched arm, the rod of Elo-
> him. . . . That rod was the symbol and pledge of His
> presence and power and working.[2]

Moses stood at the top of the hill, holding up his staff for all
to see. As they looked up, the warriors could see it high above
the battlefield, and Israel gained ground. The sight of the staff
encouraged the men in the thick of the battle. If they could not
see the rod—God's banner—then they knew their commander
had been killed and all was lost.

But Moses got tired and when his arms drooped, the enemy
surged forward once again. Something had to be done if Israel was
to win the battle. Aaron and Hur pushed up a large stone so that
Moses could sit, and then the two stood on either side of him and
held up his arms until sunset. Moses was strengthened, the entire
army was encouraged by the symbol of God's presence in Moses'

hand, and they won the battle!

After their victory, Moses built an altar and named it Yah-weh-Nissi, "The LORD is my Banner." This name means "The LORD is my sign of conquest."[3] In other words, Moses used this name to declare that God would always conquer the foes of His people. So long as Moses and the Israelites followed the Lord, they would have victory.

A Pole of Redemption

There was another time when looking up brought Israel hope. The Israelites, who were still wandering around the desert, were complaining again: "Why have you brought us up out of Egypt to die in the desert? There is no bread! There is no water! And we detest this miserable food!" (Numbers 21:5). The pattern of complaint started early in the journey and had developed into a serious problem. They spoke not only against Moses, but also against God!

It's easy for me to be critical of this until I remember that I, too, complain about how things are sometimes run, about the government, or about decisions my husband has made. In my griping, I am murmuring first against the people God has placed in leadership over me, and then against God Himself. The Israelites were sinful, imperfect people just like I am.

Because of their chronic complaining, God sent snakes among them. The serpents were poisonous and people died. Only after many deaths did the Israelites recognize their sin and ask for release from the plague. God's answer to that prayer was interesting. "The LORD said to Moses, 'Make a snake and put it up on a pole; anyone who is bitten can look at it and live'" (Numbers 21:8). So a pole with a bronze serpent was raised in the middle of the camp.

This pole foreshadowed Christ's death on the cross.

> When Moses lifted up a brazen serpent in the wilderness so that all who had been bitten by serpents might look and live, the word used for the pole on which he raised it is our word for *banner*. The Lord said to Nicodemus: "And as Moses lifted up the serpent in the wilderness, even so must the Son of Man be lifted up" (John 3:14, NASB). So the cross of Christ is our banner of God's mighty power in redemption.[4]

By looking up to the pole, the Israelites were obeying God and putting their faith in God alone for help. The snake had nothing to do with it; it was merely a symbol. Once again, God took something ordinary and gave it powerful significance. The act of looking up to God in obedience brought the Israelites salvation.

God's plan from eternity has been to provide a banner of hope for His people. Jesus said, "But I, when I am lifted up from the earth, will draw all men to myself" (John 12:32). His crucifixion was a banner raised in victory over sin's darkness for all eternity. First Corinthians 15:55-57 says, "'Where, O death, is your victory? Where, O death, is your sting?' The sting of death is sin, and the power of sin is the law. But thanks be to God! He gives us the victory through our Lord Jesus Christ." We are on the winning side! We look to the cross and know that we—and our sins—are forgiven; we are freed from the bondage of sin. A powerful truth!

Jesus' death on the cross is our assurance of God's everpresence. This symbol of victory is an eternal monument to God's grace. When we invite Jesus into our lives, it's as if we are declaring: "I am leaving what I was before and committing myself to another Master. I belong to a holy God, and He dwells in me."

But not only is the cross of Christ our banner in redemption, it is also our banner in warfare.

We Are at War

Those of us who are committed to Christ are in a battle. "For our struggle is not against flesh and blood, but against the rulers, against the authorities, against the powers of this dark world and against the spiritual forces of evil in the heavenly realms" (Ephesians 6:12). Our combat is with Satan, the ruler of the kingdom of the air and the prince of this world (Ephesians 2:2, John 12:31).

Although Satan reigns over the kingdoms of this world, God has placed His people here. We are ordinary people indwelt by the Spirit of God. When we accept Jesus into our hearts, He fills us with Himself. Now the Devil fights against God through us. It is the treasure of His presence within us that our Enemy is seeking to destroy. Commentator Matthew Henry said Satan "labors . . . to deface the heavenly image (of God) in our hearts."[5] Ultimately, however, he will not win the war. First John 4:4 tells us, "You, dear children, are from God and have overcome them, because the one who is in you is greater than the one who is in the world." The Lord is our banner—our victory is secure!

But while Satan is doomed to not win the war, he can still win the individual battles we have with temptation. Do not underestimate him; he is a master at battlefield strategy and cannot be trusted. Ironically, though, he tries to convince believers that God is the One who cannot be trusted!

The great deceiver is subtle. Have you heard someone say, "You better not ask for patience because God will send you trials"? Or, "Don't say 'O God, do anything you want with me.' He might send you to Africa!" Such comments, while often said in jest, indicate a subtle distrust of God. Such thinking is as old as the first interaction Satan had with humankind. When he talked with Eve in the garden he said, "Did God *really* say . . .?" He questioned God then—and as a human race we have been questioning Him ever since.

My friend Muriel Cook was on a plane going to Phoenix, Arizona. Just before takeoff, a beautiful woman hurried onto the plane and sat down. Muriel was reading her Bible and praying for an opportunity to speak to her seatmate. Soon after takeoff the woman turned and said, "I see you're reading your Bible. I haven't read mine in ages." Muriel asked her if she was a believer, and she said, "Yes, but I have a hole in my pants from backsliding. Right now everything is going so well in my life; I have a wonderful husband, a beautiful home, and two lovely children. I just know that God is going to take it away from me or make something awful happen if I don't get right with Him!"

It was the perfect opportunity for Muriel to share Romans 2:4 with her: "Or do you show contempt for the riches of his kindness, tolerance and patience, not realizing that God's kindness leads you toward repentance?" Her seatmate had fallen into the age-old trap of thinking that God cannot be trusted. The lovely things in her life were there because God was calling to her, longing for her to recognize His hand in the goodness around her. The Enemy had deceived her into thinking she could not trust God.

The Truth About Temptation

Satan has not changed. He attacks God's people by enticing them to sin through temptation. The more you understand temptation, the better equipped you will be to resist it.

Temptation Is Inevitable; It Is Common to All

Jesus said, "In this world you *will* have trouble" (John 16:33, emphasis added). He taught His disciples to pray, "And lead us not into temptation, but deliver us from the evil one" (Matthew 6:13). We are told that no temptation is new, it is common to all of us (1 Corinthians 10:13). That puts us all in the same category: we were all born in sin, and therefore we are all targets for temptation.

Temptation Is Morally Neutral

The Bible tells us that Christ was tempted just as we are, but was without sin (Hebrews 4:15). In other words, temptation in and of itself is not sin—what we do with it is what opens the door to sin. Satan often tempts us first with our thoughts. The thought itself—the temptation—is not a sin. But if we dwell on the temptation or act on it, we have crossed the line into sin.

We Are More Susceptible to Sin at Certain Times than at Others
Let me give you some examples:

- When I am tired at the end of a long day, it is easy for me to put my mind into neutral. That is when Satan will take advantage and plant a seed of doubt or cause a wrong thought to form.
- Vacations are also difficult for me because I let down my mental guard, and when I relax, Satan jumps in to take advantage of the situation.
- Sarah told me she is susceptible at certain times of the month because of her body's hormonal changes.
- Lynette says that the hour before dinner can be tough because her blood sugar can get low and her family is tired and rushed.
- For Jeanie, the anniversary of a painful experience, her nephew's suicide, contributes to her emotional sensitivity to temptation.

Different people have different things that heighten their susceptibility. Jesus said, "Watch and pray so that you will not fall into temptation. The spirit is willing, but the body is weak" (Matthew 26:41). We are to be alert and on the lookout, especially during these times of susceptibility.

We need to know ourselves and our weaknesses so we can be on guard against temptations. I have certain areas in which I am especially vulnerable. I call these my "pet sins." I try to avoid any situations that might cause me to be tempted in these areas—I know my weaknesses! Do you know yours? If not, ask God to help you identify your own areas of weakness. If you ask for His help, He will show you: "To the LORD I cry aloud, and he answers me" (Psalm 3:4).

When we know our weaknesses, we can ask God to remind us of our vulnerabilities, to help us to be obedient and submissive to His will. I often ask for sensitivity to the Spirit's prompting. I often inquire of Him, "Did that offend You?" "Does this please You?"

Temptation Is Dangerous and Should Not Be Courted

First Peter 5:8 states, "Your enemy the devil prowls around like a roaring lion looking for someone to devour." When we flirt with temptation, it is like placing our heads in the mouth of a roaring animal. When we are tempted, we need to remember that it means the Enemy is near. We need to say to God, "I cannot beat this. Please help me."

God Allows Satan to Tempt Us, but He Sets Limits

Satan is on a leash that God is holding. It is as if God says to the Devil, "This far and no farther." This truth is plainly seen in the book of Job. Here is the scenario: Satan tells God that Job is righteous only because of the good things God has given him. As a result, God gives Satan permission to attack Job, but He also sets limitations. In God's first interaction with Satan about Job, He says, "Very well, then, everything he has is in your hands, but on the man himself do not lay a finger" (Job 1:12). And a second time He says, "Very well, then, he is in your hands; but you must spare his life" (Job 2:6).

What can we learn from this? The Enemy tempts us, seeking to bring about our downfall, but God allows it in order to strengthen us. That can give us hope. Few things develop strength in a believer like seeking God's help in times of temptation. The prophet Isaiah recognized that when he said, "Surely it was for my benefit that I suffered such anguish. In your love you kept me from the pit of destruction; you have put all my sins behind your back" (Isaiah 38:17). First Peter 5:10 also promises that God Himself will restore us after undergoing the suffering of temptation: "And the God of all grace, who called you to his eternal glory in Christ, after you have suffered a little while, will himself restore you and make you strong, firm and steadfast."

Temptation Will Be with Us Until Death

There will never be a time in this life when we can say, "Finally, I don't have to fight this battle with temptation." I remember a young man telling us about going to the hospital to visit his mentor, an elderly, godly man. He had been a powerful man of

God; his life had been full of ministry. He was a public speaker, prayer warrior, missionary, and pastor. The gentleman was nearing death. He was in a wheelchair, unable to walk, read, or do anything for himself. It had been many weeks since he'd been able to go outdoors. The younger man was deeply shaken when his mentor said, "Since my illness, I have never wrestled so much with temptation." It was a valuable lesson. Even when we are not in public, when we are flat in bed, Satan attacks. We are locked in a battle with the Enemy of our souls until the day death ushers us into the presence of God.

The Victory Is Ours to Claim!

Our God is Yahweh-Nissi, "The Lord is our Banner." We look up to Him for victory and that gives us hope. God has won! We also need to do our part in order to walk in that victory over the Enemy.

Pray
In the Lord's Prayer, Jesus taught us to ask that we not enter into temptation. We can pray for strength to obey God and follow His Word because sin is near. We can petition God to cover and put His shield about us (Psalm 91:4, Isaiah 51:16). We can ask Him for transformation, not just deliverance: "Do not conform any longer to the pattern of this world, but be transformed by the renewing of your mind. Then you will be able to test and approve what God's will is—his good, pleasing and perfect will" (Romans 12:2). Ask God to help you renew your mind as a protection against temptation.

If you know you have sinned, pray immediately for cleansing. Not long ago I was speaking and a thought born of arrogance and pride crossed my mind. I remember thinking, *I will take care of this now.* No one around me knew what was going on; I continued speaking. But in the quiet of my heart, I acknowledged my pride and asked for forgiveness and cleansing. God is right here with us; we don't have to wait until "the right time."

Read and Memorize Scripture in Order to Resist Satan

James 4:7 says, "Resist the devil, and he will flee from you." We are able to fight against the Enemy with Scripture, the sword in the Christian's armor (Ephesians 6:17). To do this effectively, you need to read God's Word and learn to apply it to your life. The psalmist said, "I have hidden your word in my heart that I might not sin against you" (Psalm 119:11).

Memorize passages that pertain to your areas of vulnerability to sin. One of the synonyms for vulnerability is "exposed position." When the Word of God does not cover us, we are in an exposed position and Satan will take advantage of it. Hebrews 4:12 tells us, "For the word of God is living and active. Sharper than any double-edged sword, it penetrates even to dividing soul and spirit, joints and marrow; it judges the thoughts and attitudes of the heart."

When Satan tempted Jesus, His only responses were Scripture. I have taken His example to heart by memorizing verses to use as a sword when Satan tempts me in my areas of weakness. God's Spirit helps me combat the Evil One.

Several years ago I found myself caught in a pattern of wrong thinking. I was dwelling on a certain situation every time my mind wasn't engaged elsewhere. I cried out to God and asked Him to give me the strength to fight. It was extremely difficult to break the cycle because I had allowed every unoccupied moment to be taken up with this thinking. I would wake up at night, and Satan would be whispering in my ear. I would say, "God, I'm too tired to put on the armor." But because I love Him and wanted freedom from the wrong thinking, I would fight by quoting appropriate Scripture.

My friend Susie also found help from memorizing Scripture. From the time she was twelve years old, Susie wrestled with a destructive addictive habit. She had grown adept at hiding it from everyone that knew her. She had been married for many years before her husband discovered her carefully guarded secret. As the habit increased its stranglehold on her, she realized that everything she counted dear was at stake. She turned to prayer and fasting and found some relief. Then she began to memorize whole chapters and books of the Bible. When the overwhelming temptations to indulge herself came over her, she faithfully quoted Scripture in the face of the strong urges. Today, Susie is free from the terrible habit that dominated her. The power of God's Word broke the strong bonds of addictive behavior, and yet Susie still looks to God *daily* to keep from sliding back into her old pattern.

If You Can't Resist, Run

Stay as far away as possible from sin and temptation. For some, that means not going to certain movies or avoiding various types of books or magazines. For others, it could mean not walking by a bar or the candy aisle in the grocery store. It may mean not stocking certain foods in your cupboards or not spending so much time with certain people.

Teach your children also to run if they cannot resist. It is better to run than to fall into sin. First Timothy 6:11 says, "But you, [woman] of God, *flee* from all this, and pursue righteousness, godliness, faith, love, endurance and gentleness" (emphasis added).

We Need the Body of Christ to Support Us in the Battle

Remember how Aaron and Hur supported Moses by keeping his hands raised during the battle? At times we too will get tired of the fight, and we need others to come alongside us to hold up our hope and say, "Let me help you look up. Let me hold up your hands in faith. God is on the winning side, and because of that, you are, too!"

I was thirty-two years old; my children were one, four, and seven. Our lives were going well, Cal's practice was thriving, and our home was nearly always full of company. We had a wonderful church and good friends. Then one morning, Cal woke up with a blinding headache. He stumbled out of bed and struggled to get dressed. I begged him to stay in bed, but he felt he needed to do his rounds. Several hours later, in the middle of a snowstorm, he returned and practically fell into my arms. The headache had worsened. I had never seen him like that. Cal was very ill.

My talk with his fellow doctors told me that he might have something more than a simple migraine or the flu. The senior partner left his patients and quickly came to take Cal to the hospital. By that time, Cal could not sit up without excruciating pain in his head. When he was settled in a makeshift bed in the back of the doctor's car, his partner slipped up beside me and as he pointed up, said, "This is very serious, Mimi; you must pray."

Hurriedly, I farmed the children out to different friends' care and prepared to leave for the hospital. The snow was falling thickly and traveler's advisories were being broadcast on the radio and television. I inched my way to the hospital, so frozen with fear for Cal's life that I barely noticed the ice and snowdrifts that made the drive difficult.

When I got to the hospital, I learned that Cal was already being put through a series of exhaustive tests. They directed me to the basement of the large building, and as I wound my way further and further into the labyrinth of hallways, the cold seemed to penetrate my heart. I realized that they were testing Cal for a brain tumor, and that I was facing the possibility of losing the man that I had planned to spend my life with. I felt hopeless and empty.

As I sat in the bowels of the hospital, certain that I was going to be a widow at the age of thirty-two, I heard a voice say, "There you are!" One of my good friends had left her children with a baby-sitter and had braved the snowstorm to come and sit with me. Soon another friend arrived. As I sat there, flanked by the two women, I realized that their coming had encouraged me. Their presence and their faith were to me what I am sure Aaron and Hur were to Moses. They urged me to look up to my heavenly Father on Cal's behalf, and hope flooded my heart. When I looked up, I was reminded that God was in charge and that I could trust Him with everything that pertained to those whom I love.

After two months of complete bed rest, Cal's problem was diagnosed as a facial fracture. His spinal fluid was draining through his Eustachian tube into his throat. An experimental treatment was tried and it worked. Over the past twenty-one years, Cal's fracture has remained sealed. We have been told that it could break open at any time. Each time that thought comes into my mind, I find my soul clinging tightly to Yahweh-Nissi, my Hope.

Trust

Remember to look daily to Yahweh-Nissi. He is your hope and help. The Cross stands forever in eternity as the final victory over Satan. Through Him we are more than conquerors (Romans 8:37).

Kathy was in emotional pain and she felt hopeless. Her young son, Bert, was incorrigible. At least once a week and sometimes more, the school called Kathy and her husband because Bert had once again gotten in trouble. Early each morning, Kathy awakened to pray about Bert and his future. Every time the phone rang, she cringed, certain that someone else was calling with bad news about Bert's behavior. She began having nightmares, dreaming that Bert was in the penitentiary. As her fear and despair over Bert grew, Kathy began to suffer severe stomach pain and often lived with nausea all day long. One day she acknowledged to a friend that she had lost hope for her son.

Her friend told her that she wasn't trusting God. Kathy felt hurt at first, but on further reflection she began to see that her faithful prayer times had been worry sessions that she invited God to listen in on. She had been looking at Bert's behavior and had not been looking up to God. Her prayers for her son began to change. Daily she affirmed her faith in God's promise that He had begun a good work in Bert, and He would finish it. Kathy told God that she was choosing to trust Him to take care of Bert; that she was placing the boy in His hands. She stood on the fact that God had given Bert to them and there was no mistake. Hope and health returned as Kathy looked to God and not to her circumstances. God gave Kathy hope when she looked to Him, even when she had no assurance that things would change.

If Kathy had no assurance that things would change, how could she have hope? What if her son was put in jail? What if he lost his life? Kathy's choice to change her focus and trust God meant that she was choosing to stand on the ultimate victory that Christ won on the cross. If she was looking to God, she could accept jail, and even death, as a part of His plan for Bert. She took to heart Paul's powerful statement in Romans 8:38, "For I am convinced that neither death nor life, neither angels nor demons, neither the present nor the future, nor any powers, neither height nor depth, nor anything else in all creation, will be able to separate us from the love of God that is in Christ Jesus our Lord." That verse gave her hope that nothing that happened to Bert would be out of God's reach. She declared out loud and often, "I know *whom* I have believed and am convinced that he is able to guard what I have entrusted to him for that day" (2 Timothy 1:12, emphasis added). She had entrusted Bert's entire life and future to God and that gave her hope.

Most of us face situations that seem hopeless. Most of us wrestle with questions that seemingly have no answers. When we look up to Yahweh-Nissi, He gives hope. He gives us hope because He is the victor over Satan. He gives us hope because He looks over time and promises that "all things work together for good" (Romans 8:28). We can live each day looking to Him for all we need to face the difficulties of life. When we have Jesus, we can live intentionally with hope each day.

Remembering the God of Hope

When we live intentionally, there are some things we can do to remind ourselves that God is Yahweh-Nissi, the God of hope.

HOLY HABIT:
Build altars of remembrance.

Most of what we have talked about in the development of holy habits has to do with noticing and remembering. Moses and Gideon both built altars as a way to remember the victories that God gave them. When we notice and remember, then we can let the truths of what we have seen make us soft before Yahweh-Nissi. Many of the victories we enjoy in our lives are private, but we can use certain things to remind us of what God has done. Here are some examples:

- When I drive by a certain house, I am reminded of past hurts that God healed. That place has become an altar to the victory of healing in my life. Whenever I drive by, it reminds me to be thankful to God for what He has done.
- Shelly asked God to provide for fabric to re-cover their couch. She wrestled with discouragement over their limited resources. One day the fabric store down the street from her parents' home had an unannounced fifty-percent-off sale. She was able to buy beautiful material. Every time she sits on the couch she is reminded that God answered her prayer. It is a call to thankfulness.
- The pew at church where I led a woman to Christ is an altar of remembrance. It reminds me to rejoice that she is growing in the grace of God.

HOLY HABIT:
SHARE SPIRITUAL VICTORIES YOU AND OTHERS HAVE EXPERIENCED.

Oftentimes we are cheered by God's victory in our own lives, but we don't rejoice at the victories that members of the body of Christ are experiencing all over the world. When anyone who belongs to Christ experiences a victory, it is ours too. That is true because as believers, we are part of the same body. We belong to the same Lord. God's victory on behalf of one of His children is a victory for everyone who is His! Because He is the God who never changes, that means that He can work victory for us, too! As with other kinds of joy, shared victories help me see that God is working on every front and winning. If I revel in the victories of those around me, there is much more joy than one person can handle.

Recently we invited some retired missionaries to our home to watch a video put out by the New Tribes Mission. The film showed how an entire tribe accepted Christ all at once. I had watched it twice before we invited our friends. The second time,

I watched it on my knees, thanking God for His victory over evil. I had the joy of watching the faces of these veteran missionaries as they rejoiced to see an entire tribe dancing over the joy of salvation.

✳

I ALSO COLLECT STORIES THAT REMIND ME OF GOD'S VICTORIES. A middle-aged missionary couple in Spain with whom I visited told me the following story. Several years ago, they had met an older woman in the city square. The lady had spent thirty years in missionary service in the African country of Senegal. The couple invited her to their home for rest and refreshment. As this woman talked, it became apparent that she had suffered. She said she felt that her years of service had been wasted. She lost one son to a crocodile, another son had been seriously ill, and her husband died. When she left Senegal, a grieving widow and mother, there had not been one convert to show for the sacrifices of thirty years.

During their visit, the couple mentioned that they had recently received a newsletter from some young friends, also missionaries in Senegal. They shared the newsletter with her, and as she read it, she began to cry. The letter told of how the young couple had contacted different tribes. They were surprised to discover an amazing God-consciousness among them. Their view of God as Father was so clear, and the young couple said they had no idea where it had come from. People from seven different tribes were coming to Christ. When the retired missionary lifted her head from the letter, she said, "Our family lived and ministered among five of the seven tribes mentioned in this letter. We never knew if they understood. But now I know!"

Yahweh-Nissi is winning one battle after another. In our fight in this world, let's not forget to attend the victory parties. God is triumphant, and for that reason, we have hope.

PRAYER

God of all grace,
Whose thoughts toward us are ever thoughts of peace and not of
evil, give us hearts to believe that we are accepted in the Beloved;
and give us minds to admire that perfection of moral wisdom
which found a way to preserve the integrity of heaven and yet
receive us there.
We are astonished and marvel that one so
holy and dread should invite us into
Thy banqueting house and cause love to
be the banner over us.
We cannot express the gratitude we feel,
but look Thou on our hearts and read it there.
Amen.[6]

S T U D Y   A N D   D I S C U S S I O N Q U E S T I O N S

1. Read Ephesians 6:10-18, then fill out the chart below.

The armor used	How the lack of this piece affects our mind	How the lack of this piece affects our hope

2. Psalm 39:7 and Romans 15:13 make statements of hope. Write your own statement based on what you have gleaned from this chapter on daily hope.

3. Read Romans 12:12 and 2 Thessalonians 2:16-17. What are we called to include in our hope? How do you think we can do that based on what we have studied?

4. According to 1 Peter 1:3, what does "living hope" come from? How is it different from ordinary hope? What are we to do with our hope? (See 1 Peter 1:13, 3:15.)

5. Read Luke 5:18-20. How are the friends of the paralytic like Aaron and Hur in the Old Testament? Why was the man healed? What conclusions can we draw from this story about our faith on behalf of others?

6. Make a list of the times when you find temptation strongest; for example, when your hormonal levels are varied or during certain seasons of life. What steps can you take to avoid or resist temptation in each situation?

7. You may not want to share your "pet sins" out loud, but make a private list of your weaknesses. Seek out verses that will help you combat these areas of vulnerability. If possible, find a trusted believer who is willing to hold you accountable in these areas and will support you in prayer.

8. Read 1 Corinthians 10:13. How have you found these truths to be worked out in your own life?

9. Read James 1:12-18. Rewrite these verses in your own words.

10. Because trust is a key part of claiming victory, read Psalm 9:10 and reflect on the various names of God that we have studied so far. How has your trust in God changed through a deeper understanding of His names?

CHAPTER EIGHT

Living in Peace

Yahweh-Shalom

*J*RACED TO THE BACK DOOR WITH MY PURSE THROWN OVER MY shoulder and a child under each arm. No, this was not a fire alarm! It was just my typical exit into a busy day. As usual, I did not have time to let two toddlers walk to the car on their own. My responses to my children's many questions were short and to the point. As I drove, I prayed, "Lord make all the stoplights green!"

When people asked me how I was, I gave short answers: "busy," "in a tear," "flying," or "hanging in there." I felt a great deal of satisfaction when I was able to check everything off the to-do list for that day. I was so intent on accomplishing things for God that I was easily irritated with anyone in my circle of influence who made a mistake. For example, if a child spilled a glass of milk at dinner, I would snap at them in rebuke. After all, now I had to spend precious time cleaning up the mess! But at the same time, if one of them told a lie, I couldn't take the time to stop and deal with it, except to say, "Don't say that." I was sending a message that anything was all right as long as Mom didn't have to slow down to deal with it. By example, I was teaching my family the wrong things.

All around me God was offering the treasures of heaven, and I was too busy to savor any part of His kindness. First I was too busy accomplishing and then I became busy in my search for who I wanted to become. When I began studying the lives of great Christians, I wanted everything they had . . . now! But the only way I could think of attaining that was to move into higher gear. But the faster I moved, the less control I had over everything in my life. When you're running a race, you can sprint because the race only lasts a short time. But when you sprint day in and day out, you use up what God has supplied for emergencies. I was tapping into my reserves in order to get through each day; as a result I was close to burnout.

One day I asked our son Kurt to run and get me something. He looked at me seriously and asked, "Mom, would it be all right if I walked?" I was horrified to see that my children were feeling the brunt of my frantic lifestyle. Sure, I was accomplishing a lot—but for whom and at what cost? The rush of life was taking its toll on me and those around me.

I had been interviewing elderly people about what they had learned in life, and their words began to penetrate my heart. Many told me, "I wished my life away." I, too, found myself wishing that certain commitments I had made would be over. I wished that my children were older, wished that I had not joined a certain organization, or that whatever season we were in was over. I found that even though I had accepted certain responsibilities, I didn't want to have anything to do with them! I was in a constant state of disquiet and unrest, but I felt that God had gifted me and that I was responsible to use my gifts for Him. How could I slow down and be a woman of peace *and* an obedient servant?

God had given me a lot of energy and good health so that I could be productive, but in order to be able to do things well, I needed emotional calmness. To me, emotional calmness meant not only being pleasant on the outside, but also having a quietness of soul and spirit within. Over time, I learned ways to help me slow down.

Ironically, as my soul grew quieter, I began to see that my frantic activity and emotional intensity had been covering up a huge void. There was an indescribable longing within me. I felt incomplete. There was a lack of spiritual well-being, a restlessness. I even experienced physical symptoms, almost like nausea, an empty hollowness from my chest to my stomach. There was a craving. My soul was dry and barren. It was as if I had been running a machine with no oil; my spirit ground on itself, it squeaked and grated. I needed an infinite God to fill the infinite hole inside my heart. No amount of effort on my part would change me. Only the God of peace could turn me into a woman of peace.

As I prayed for Him to change me, I turned my focus to knowing more about why He is called Yahweh-Shalom, The LORD is Peace. I soon learned that Scripture speaks of both peace with God and the peace of God. Both are necessary to fully experience God's peace in this life.

Peace *with* God

The nation of Israel was in upheaval. Because they had rebelled against God, He had given the Israelites into the hands of the Midianites. For seven years these Bedouin raiders cruelly oppressed them, throwing the country into turmoil: "They camped on the land and ruined the crops all the way to Gaza and did not spare a living thing for Israel, neither sheep nor cattle nor donkeys" (Judges 6:4). The land was so ravaged that the Israelites were hiding in caves in fear for their lives. If ever there had been a need for peace, it was at this point in Israel's history. They had gone from one foreign occupation to another. They were no longer their own people. Despite all that God had done for them in the past, they had turned their backs on Him. "Israel knew no peace because it no longer knew God's presence."[1] Things got so desperate that they finally called upon God for help.

When the angel of the Lord went to visit Gideon, he was

threshing wheat in a winepress. Wheat threshing was normally done outside where the wind could catch the chaff and dust and carry it away. The winepress was indoors, unventilated, but safe from the scrutiny of the enemy. Gideon wanted to keep the wheat from the Midianites (verse 11). He wasn't about to be discovered with something that had escaped their notice. While Gideon was threshing, the angel of the Lord appeared and greeted him, "The LORD is with you, mighty warrior" (verse 12). This didn't seem to make sense to Gideon. He replied, "But sir . . . if the LORD is with us, why has all this happened to us? Where are all his wonders that our fathers told us about?" (verse 13). Gideon was looking for tangible evidence of God's presence, almost like a good luck charm. Gideon hadn't let God get ahold of him yet. He couldn't believe his ears—especially when the angel told him that God had appointed him to save Israel from the Midianites. All he knew was that his family wasn't important and he was the least signifi-cant of his humble clan.

Gideon knew that as a good host, he had to provide something for the angel. He asked for an opportunity to prepare an offering. Gideon was generous with the portions, especially considering the difficulty they were having in securing food during those hard days. He served meat, broth, and bread . . . but the angel, instead of eating the food, touched it with a staff and everything burned up! It was the consuming fire that convinced Gideon that he had been in the presence of the Sovereign Lord. This frightened him, but God spoke and said, "I will be with you" (verse 16). It was after the encounter with the angel and God's promise of His pres-ence that Gideon built an altar and named it Yahweh-Shalom, "The LORD is Peace" (verse 24). "This peace included not only his personal welfare, but also the restoration of Israel's freedom and prosperity."[2]

Even though he had the assurance that The LORD is Peace, Gideon was still afraid. He tore down his father's altar to the pagan god at night because he feared his family. Then, when he had gathered the army together, he still wasn't sure that God was going to give him victory, and he asked God twice to give him a sign. After God had winnowed Gideon's troops down to only three hundred men, He told Gideon to attack and that victory would be theirs. Then He said, "If you are afraid to attack, go down to the camp with your servant Purah and listen to what they are saying. Afterward you will be encouraged to attack the camp" (Judges 7:10-11). Sure enough, Gideon overheard a Midianite soldier telling a friend about a dream he had. The interpretation of the dream promised victory to Gideon's army. When Gideon heard this, he returned to his camp a new man. Listen to his words: "Get up! The LORD has given the Midianite camp into your hands. . . . Watch me. . . . Follow my lead. When I get to the edge of the camp, do exactly as I do" (verses 15,17). Is this the same man who had told God, "My clan is the weakest in Manasseh, and I am the least in my family" (6:15)? Despite Gideon's doubts and fears, God kept His promise to him. Gideon had become the mighty warrior that the angel had prophetically called him.

After the battle, the Israelites asked Gideon to rule over them. He replied, "The LORD will rule over you" (Judges 8:23). From all we can tell, that was the smartest thing he did in his entire life. When Israel looked to God as their leader—reconciling their relationship with Him—they enjoyed peace for forty years.

When we think of peace, an image of quietness, calmness, and a lack of conflict come to mind, but the biblical definition is much fuller. *Shalom* implies "wholeness, a harmony of relationship with God, or reconciliation. It expressed the deepest desire and need of the human heart. It represented the greatest measure of contentment and satisfaction in life."[3]

Israel experienced peace as a nation when they reconciled with God and enjoyed the restoration of relationship. This is not only true on a national level, but also on a personal one. King David is one of the strongest biblical examples of this truth. He enjoyed such intimate fellowship with God that he was known as a man after God's heart (1 Samuel 13:14, Acts 13:22). But David failed to resist temptation, and he made a series of sinful choices, each one taking him further away from God.

When David indulged his lust and slept with Bathsheba, another man's wife, he became tangled in sin's web. The web tightened when he heard the news that Bathsheba was pregnant, and because her husband Uriah had been on the battlefield, it was impossible that he could be the father. In an effort to cover up his sin, David gave orders for Uriah to come home, all the while hoping he would make love with Bathsheba and not suspect the adultery when she told him she was expecting. But David's plans for cover-up failed when Uriah refrained from having sexual relations with his wife. By this time, David was so afraid of being found out, and so hardhearted, that he gave orders for Uriah to be murdered! He was so far from God that he didn't even acknowledge his sin until the prophet Nathan confronted him.

David wrote Psalm 51 after he had broken the sweet communion that he'd known with his Lord. This psalm reflects the incredible turmoil and lack of peace he was experiencing. I once heard someone say you only know how far you are from God if you have known nearness to Him. Only a person who had been close to God could have written Psalm 51. "Have mercy on me, O God, according to your unfailing love; according to your great compassion blot out my transgressions" (verse 1). David understood that God deeply loves His children in spite of their rebellion. But much of David's psalm reflects a lack of inner peace, a disquieted mind: "My sin is always before me" (verse 3). His mind obviously was caught by what he had done. Disharmony even affects us physically; I often feel an achiness in my body when my spirit has no peace. David said that his bones were "crushed."

Although David's sin might have been acceptable in his culture, there was something else needed for peace to reign in the heart of one who was known as a "man after God's own heart." The standard for peace with God comes from God Himself. Three times David asked for cleansing (verses 2,7,10). He desperately longed for all to be made right. In essence he was pleading, "Cleanse me of my sin, make me really clean, make me new from within. Don't just clean me up, transfuse me with Your blood." He knew that his heart was steeped in sin.

A person in the cleaning business once told me that if a stain goes all the way through a fabric, it will not come out. This has been helpful as a housekeeping tip, but it also has a spiritual application. If you could turn your heart over, you would find the effects of sin clear through. To be right with God, we need something new and fresh. That's why David begged God to "*create in me a pure heart*" (verse 10, emphasis added). He was asking for a heart that has a faithful, steadfast, and willing spirit, one that would consistently and eagerly want to please his Lord and Master.

David would have done anything to be restored to a right relationship with God. He wrote, "You do not delight in sacrifice, or I would bring it; you do not take pleasure in burnt offerings. The sacrifices of God are a broken spirit; a broken and contrite heart, O God, you will not despise" (verses 16-17). When our relationship with God is broken, what can we give Him if He does not want our sacrifices? We can give Him a heart bent in submission, one that seeks relationship in softness and gentleness with Him.

Our prayer should be "God, I offer to you a soft heart." Sin hardens the heart. It is an infraction, a violation of the holiness of God; it is like breaking a contract. When we sin, we must go to Him in repentance, seeking reconciliation.

It is impossible to have peace with God apart from confession of sin and repentance. But as my own life illustrated, peace *with* God does not guarantee that we will enjoy the peace *of* God, and God longs for His children to have both.

The Peace *of* God

The peace of God—an inner settling, a calmness of soul despite our circumstances or activities—is achieved only when our needs are filled with wholeness and a harmony of relationship with God. My mental image of this is that my soul is connected to a pipeline. That pipeline is God. When I am reconciled to God, all that is from Him flows through me—but only if I am looking to Him. I have to be connected to the pipeline. There are many things that can contribute to a lack of or break in harmony with God.

In Matthew 14 we read that Jesus put the disciples into a boat so He could pray alone. While the disciples were crossing to the other side, a storm came up and they were being tossed about on the lake. Jesus came to them walking on the water. It was unusual that Jesus would walk to them on the water, but the fact that it was the middle of the night added to their terror. Surely a ghost was coming toward their boat!

The passage says, "But Jesus *immediately* said to them: 'Take courage! It is I. Don't be afraid'" (Matthew 14:27, emphasis added). He did not let them stew in their fear. His assurance was immediate. Peter decided that if it really was the Lord, He could make him walk on the water too! So he asked permission and Jesus simply said, "Come." As Peter was walking on the water he took his eyes off Jesus and saw the wind. As the waves slapped up against his legs, Peter, the big seaman, was gripped with fear. "Lord, save me!" he cried. And again the Bible says that Jesus *immediately* reached out and caught Peter. Once Peter's hand was in the Lord's, peace reigned again.

Peter lost the peace of God because he focused on his circumstances rather than on the source of peace. As I studied this aspect of God's character, He showed me that I had not been experiencing the peace of God because He had not been my focus, either. I had been focused on serving God, and even though my focus seemed good and worthy, it was not sufficient. I was not connected to the pipeline. You may not be experiencing the peace of God because you, too, have focused on other things: your circumstances, a marriage where there is no unity, a lack of fulfillment in your job, conflicts with your relatives or neighbors, or financial pressures on every side. Maybe you are even struggling to meet society's standards and are preoccupied with how you should look.

When we lose our focus on God, we unhook our souls from the pipeline of God's character. We are without a lifeline. Unrest and lack of peace is the result. If you are overcome by the waves of your life, a call to Yahweh-Shalom, which refocuses your *attention*, can restore wholeness with Him immediately.

Carla was the successful manager of an exclusive dress shop. She had grown up in a wealthy, religious family. Top priority in her childhood home was church attendance and proper outward behavior. But the messages she got were always mixed. Her father, who was one of the best Sunday school teachers in the church, was a cheat and liar in his business dealings. Her maternal grandfather had affairs, but faithfully attended services and gave generously and ostentatiously. Because of the discrepancy in the lives of the role models around her, Carla decided that she would pursue the knowledge of God, but she did not want to open herself up for intimacy with Him. She threw herself into study of the Bible; she knew the Scriptures and doctrine, but she didn't know God. By accepting Christ as her Savior she had taken a step toward relationship, but it had stopped there and became a mental exercise, not an emotional one.

Carla's professional success distracted her from recognizing the gnawing in her heart. Every award and accolade she received, she took as her due. She did not recognize that they were gifts from God, signs of His pursuit of her heart. Her growing accomplishments increased the emptiness in her life. She had thought greater success would mean greater satisfaction.

Carla's intellectual approach to her religion spilled over into other areas of her life. She shut herself off emotionally from her husband and child. Slowly she alienated them. Every time her husband or daughter sought her emotional support, she withdrew almost in anger.

When the void inside began to consume her, it dawned on her that she had shut off her emotions at great cost. She had nearly lost her faith and her family. Her first tentative steps toward emotional connection with God were stumbling at best, but He met her in her attempts to find Him. It was as though, by faith, she would put a foot out into thin air and God would bring the ground up under her. As she opened herself up to Christ, she began to open herself to those around her. As she grew in her capacity to emotionally connect with God, she grew in her capacity to love others as well. As her relationships deepened and were healed, she experienced a peace she had not known before.

God waited a long time for Carla to come to Him. Because God is outside our human time, the point in time of our seeking Him is not critical. He can wait forever. But He wants us to come to Him. His patience with us is another sign of His great love for His children. He does not write us off! As 2 Chronicles 30:9 says, "He will not turn his face from you if you return to him."

Nehemiah expressed his awe at God's compassion when he looked back at the behavior of the children of Israel: "Stubbornly they turned their backs on you, became stiff-necked and refused to listen. For many years you were patient with them. By your Spirit you admonished them through your prophets. . . . But in your great mercy you did not put an end to them or abandon them, for you are a gracious and merciful God" (Nehemiah 9:29-31). God is patient with us. However, each day that we wait to return to God, we lose out on another day of unity with Him. We deny God another day of the joy that He receives in that oneness.

How can you and I experience God's peace? First by making sure that we have peace with God, and then by keeping the Prince of Peace as our focus.

Daily Wholeness and Harmony

You can establish some holy habits that will keep your focus on Yahweh-Shalom, the God of Peace. Here are some that help me.

HOLY HABIT:
REGULARLY EXAMINE YOUR HEART.

If we are to have harmony—peace—in our relationship with God, we must examine our hearts daily to see if we have allowed anything to disrupt that relationship with Him—conscious or unconscious: "Search me, O God, and know my heart; test me and know my anxious thoughts. See if there is any offensive [sinful] way in me" (Psalm 139:23-24). This prayer can become a daily habit. We must cultivate sensitivity to God's voice and touch on our lives. Then, when He indicates there is something wrong, we can confess it, ask for forgiveness, and ask that His peace control our hearts. God's peace is not the lack of conflict, but that which "transcends all understanding" (Philippians 4:7). It is peace in spite of what's going on around us because our focus is on Yahweh-Shalom, the author of peace, and not on the overwhelming circumstances.

HOLY HABIT:
DAILY SEEK GOD AND MAINTAIN A CONSTANT CONNECTION WITH HIM.

If we seek peace and intimacy with God each day, we won't experience the major breech in relationship with Him that King David and Carla experienced. But often we can go days, sometimes weeks, before we realize that the sweet communion we have experienced with God has been disrupted.

Sandy had been a pastor's wife for a long time. She was normally calm and easygoing, but Sandy was upset. She found herself yelling at her kids more than usual. She was short with her husband and even snapped at the church secretary. One afternoon as the shadows of the setting sun lengthened on her kitchen wall, Sandy woke up to the fact that she hadn't had a long talk with God in several weeks. She had been super busy, going to bed late each night and struggling to get out of bed in time to get the kids off to school. There just hadn't been any time to be quiet with Him. The next morning, Sandy pulled herself out of bed early, determined to get back into her devotional routine. She just couldn't seem to pick up with God where she had left off. Finally she said, "God, what is it? Is there something in my life that is keeping me from fellowship with you?"

She had learned that God was faithful to point out things in her life that kept her from intimacy with Him. That was when she remembered that her husband had come home from a church board meeting several weeks earlier, hurt and upset by something one of the elders had said. She had taken on the grievance for him and it had festered just below her consciousness. Then she realized that was why she had been so short with her family and the church secretary. When she allowed wrong attitudes to creep in, it ruptured the relationship she had with God and even the peace she enjoyed with her husband and children. She quickly confessed her wrong attitudes and laid her hurt at Jesus' feet. Once again, she was in right relationship and at peace.

HOLY HABIT:
Find your level of calmness.

When I realized that our entire family was in a stew because my life was frantic, I determined to discover how to operate within the framework of time and strength that God had given me. I chose to find the level of activity at which I could operate effectively and still maintain a spirit of peace and calmness. I needed to be peaceful in order for my family to experience peace.

To find my level of calmness, I mentally drew a circle around my inner person and another circle around that. I called the outer circle my border, or my buffer. To me, the border was like having emotional spare change in my pocket. If I were asked to do something, I would consider whether or not it was worth spending the energy, my emotional spare change. I slowly learned to cut out anything that raised the level of emotional turmoil and activity in my life so that I could walk calmly through the day.

Level of Calmness

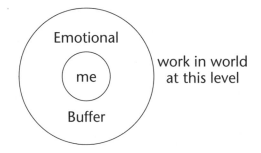

My long-term objective was to run well throughout my lifetime. In order to last, I had to find out what level of activity I could sustain over the long haul. I learned to keep my finger on my emotional pulse. I would watch for times when my heart would race out of anxiety or fear. I learned to pay attention to what I was feeling. If I felt anxious, what was causing it? A misplaced priority or a self-imposed level of busyness? Was it because I had overcommitted myself that day? If I was fearful, was my fear realistic? What was the truth about the fearful feelings? Could I do anything about it? Was I angry? What was the reason for the anger? What could I do to deal with it?

HOLY HABIT:

BECOME A COMMUNICATOR OF PEACE TO OTHERS.

Because one of my lifetime goals was to be a woman who lived with a peaceful spirit, a product of that process was the birth of a desire to have our home be an oasis. An oasis is a peaceful place, safe from the buffeting winds of life. I began to seek ways to create a sense of harmony and wholeness in our home that would be clearly communicated to those who entered it. I fill our house with lovely music. The peaceful strains speak a strong message. I will invite a stressed-out friend to come for dinner and meet her at the door with a robe and an announcement that there is some special bubble bath by the freshly scrubbed tub. She is to soak and relax until she is advised that dinner is on the table.

Stop and pray with people when they share a worry or concern, no matter where you are, even if you're speaking on the telephone. Peace often comes when we help others look to God. Ask God's Spirit to fill your home with His peace so that it permeates every nook. Look for creative ways to touch others with the peace that you enjoy within.

Any disquiet in my soul can be met moment-by-moment with the peace that comes from seeking to be connected with God. He is the God of Peace who longs for a relationship with me. He rejoices when I recognize those things that keep me from enjoying peace with Him. He is the loving Father waiting for me to turn my heart to Him. He is my Father who runs to receive me when I am repentant, and He restores me to relationship with Him because I belong to Him. As I look to Him to provide wisdom and strength for each day, He helps me find my level of calmness.

PRAYER

My Great Prince of Peace,
You have promised perfect peace if my mind,
imaginations, and affections are stayed on You.
I need daily reconciliation as my passions wander so quickly.
My fickleness is more a surprise to me than
it is to You. This moment I want to be restored.
Help me to want You the next time.
Thank You, my Gracious Father.
Amen.

STUDY AND DISCUSSION QUESTIONS

1. Have you known the nearness of God? If not, why? If so, how would you describe the peace that nearness brings?

2. Where does peace with God come from according to Isaiah 53:5, Romans 5:1, and Ephesians 2:14? How was that peace made?

3. The Bible makes it clear that we are to pursue peace (Psalm 34:14, Isaiah 27:5, Colossians 3:15). Write down the phrases from the verses given that indicate the believer's duty to seek peace.

4. With what does Psalm 29:11 say God will bless His people? Are God's blessings merited? What does that mean that peace is?

5. According to Psalm 119:165, who enjoys peace? What kind of peace is it? What is the promise made to those who enjoy peace? If we have peace, how does that promise work itself out in a difficult world?

6. Isaiah 26:3 says there is perfect peace. Who gets that perfect peace? If perfect peace comes from a mind anchored in God, how can you get your mind centered on Him?

7. We may have read John 14:27 and 16:33 many times. Why don't those verses give us lasting comfort? What does Jesus say in them about peace? What do you need to do to experience what He offers?

8. One aspect of the fruit of God's work in us is peace (Galatians 5:22-23). What is needed in your life for the "fruit of peace" to be felt?

9. What does Philippians 4:7 say will guard our hearts and minds? What are some things that aid in finding that, according to Philippians 4:4-6? How does Romans 8:6 contribute to this concept?

10. To find your level of calmness, make a list of the stressors in your life. Then note what you can change, and create a plan to do that. Write a description of what your level of calmness would be.

Holy Habits

God Is Elohim

HOLY HABIT:
"Hook" yourself to His transcendence.

HOLY HABIT:
Look for His fingerprints in the world and tell others what you see.

HOLY HABIT:
Acknowledge His power.

HOLY HABIT:
Celebrate Elohim.

God Is Yahweh

HOLY HABIT:
Remember that He is a big God.

HOLY HABIT:
Recognize each day as a gift box from God.

HOLY HABIT:
Discipline your mind.

HOLY HABIT:
Dwell on His love for you.

God Is Yahweh-Jireh

HOLY HABIT:
Ask God to teach you what His gifts to you are each day.

HOLY HABIT:
Thank Him every day.

HOLY HABIT:
Remind yourself that God's grace never runs out.

HOLY HABIT:
Tell God what you need.

God Is Yahweh-Shammah

HOLY HABIT:
Silence your heart daily so that you can be sensitive to God's presence.

HOLY HABIT:
Ask God to help you see life through His eyes.

HOLY HABIT:
Talk to God throughout the day.

God Is Yahweh-Rophe

HOLY HABIT:
Cleanse your heart daily.

HOLY HABIT:
Avoid those things that distract you from a God-centered life.

HOLY HABIT:
Seek to demonstrate your choice to forgive those who have wronged you.

God Is Yahweh-Nissi

HOLY HABIT:
Build altars of remembrance.

HOLY HABIT:
Share spiritual victories you and others have experienced.

God Is Yahweh-Shalom

HOLY HABIT:
Regularly examine your heart.

HOLY HABIT:
Daily seek God and maintain a constant connection with Him.

HOLY HABIT:
Find your level of calmness.

HOLY HABIT:
Become a communicator of peace to others.

HIS PART:
Changing Us
from the Inside Out

CHAPTER NINE

Power to Do What We Cannot

Becoming Holy

A FRIEND OF MINE VACATIONED IN ENGLAND THIS SUMMER AND spent several days in Bath. While there, she visited the national costume and clothing museum that contains an amazing array of period clothing and tapestries, each made by hand. Intricate designs and rich textures, created solely with needle and thread, transformed otherwise mundane fabrics into beautiful articles of clothing. Today they are displayed in climate- and light-controlled rooms as rare works of art, priceless in their beauty and uniqueness. Imagine, no two articles of clothing ever looked alike—and all took hundreds of hours to complete, stitch by stitch.

Even as recently as pioneer times in the United States, women spent hours stitching and sewing for their homes and families. Up at dawn, a woman worked hard all day to cook, clean, and care for her family. In the evenings after her children were tucked in bed, she would often sit in a chair pulled close to the only source of light to do her handwork. Her eyes strained to see the painstaking stitches in the light of the oil-burning lamp. Many times it was late at night before she would finally fold her work and slip off to bed. It became common to refer to intricate pieces of handiwork with the words "it smells of the lamp," meaning someone had labored long and carefully.

As Christians, we are the unique handiwork of God. Do we "smell of the lamp" of God? Have we allowed Him to create an intricate and beautiful design out of the fabric of our lives?

In the previous chapters we have looked at our part, at what we can do to keep our focus on God and make His character real to us. In this section, we will take a look at God's part—His handiwork, what He does in us—as we focus on Him.

God planned that Christ would come to earth to take us home, to be with Him and become part of His family. We are to bear His image and have His name as ours. This plan was born in the heart of God before time was created. Let that wondrous truth sink deeply into your soul: "History is not a random kaleidoscope of disconnected events; it is a process directed by the God who sees the end *in* the beginning."[1]

This God to whom we belong, who sees everything, had a plan that would call all men to an intimate relationship with Him: "'The time is coming,' declares the LORD, 'when I will make a new covenant . . . this is the covenant I will make . . . I will put my law in their minds and write it on their hearts. I will be their God, and they will be my people" (Jeremiah 31:31-33).

The word *covenant* had been used to describe the relationship between God and man. It was a contract into which man and God entered. The Old Testament believers kept their part of the old covenant by obeying the Law. However, the new covenant, the one Jesus was to make when He came to earth, was not based on the Law but on love. When we are faced with the choice of entering into covenant relationship with God, we can only accept or reject God's offer. He is responsible for the covenant: "Our relationship with God is given to us solely on the initiative and solely on the grace of God."[2]

The difference between the two covenants has a significant impact on us today. The Law was written on tablets of stone and, under the old covenant, the relationship that people had with God was based on His justice, His enforcement of the Law. It was given externally. But when God gave us the new covenant, He said that He was going to put the Law "in their minds and write it on their hearts" (Jeremiah 31:33). The concept must have been radical for those who heard Jeremiah's words! "[God] once wrote the laws *to* them, now he will write his laws *in* them. . . . The whole habit and frame of their souls shall be a table and transcript of the law of God."[3]

The words "I will be their God and they will be my people" signal an incredible difference in how God will relate to humankind. Love pulses through every word of this declaration. God promises to write the covenant in the most tender part of our being, the heart. The new covenant is an internal one. With the new covenant, our loving Father reached out with His "everlasting arms" to gather His children to Himself. God didn't want His children to obey Him simply because of the Law. He wanted obedience based on love. That's what Jesus meant when He said, "If anyone loves me, he will obey my teaching. My Father will love him, and we will come to him and make our home with him" (John 14:23). In other words, the people of the new covenant belong to God from the inside out.

Before the gift of the new covenant, God's people had access to Him only through the priest. But because of Christ's death on the cross, God's children can have direct access to Him. In that unbroken access, He pulls us toward Himself with cords of love:

> The new relationship is based entirely on the love of God. . . . The new covenant puts men into relationship with a God, who is still a God of justice, but a God whose justice has been swallowed up in His love. The most tremendous thing about the new covenant was that it made man's relationship to God no longer dependent on man's obedience. It became entirely dependent on God's love.[4]

Author and speaker Brennan Manning described the new covenant in more contemporary terms:

> Over a hundred years ago in the Deep South, a phrase
> so common in our Christian Culture today, *born again,*
> was seldom or never used. Rather, the phrase used to
> describe the breakthrough into a personal relationship
> with Jesus Christ was, "I was seized by the power of a
> great affection." These words describe both the initiative
> of God and the explosion within the heart when Jesus
> . . . becomes real, alive, and the Lord of one's personal
> and professional life.[5]

Seized by the power of a great affection. I love that!

Forever One

As God's deep love woos us, His Word speaks to us afresh. At least this has been true for me. I saw Jesus' discourse in John 15 in a new light as the wonder of God's incredible love for me began to break over me.

I had been deeply conscious of a profound need within my heart. I wanted more from God than I was experiencing. For years I had tried to stuff everything I could think of into that place. I tried to fill it with activities, friends, my marriage, and our children, but nothing satisfied that part of me. I read my Bible and prayed. But something was missing.

Throughout history, wise people have recognized this longing in the human heart. Saint Augustine and Pascal both spoke of it. This need is the place within all of humankind that was designed by God for His residence. No wonder the needs seem infinite and can't be filled! It's because infinite needs can be met only by an infinite God.

In John 15, Jesus explains how God can fill that need. He says:

> "I am the true vine, and my Father is the gardener.
> He cuts off every branch in me that bears no fruit,

while every branch that does bear fruit he prunes so
that it will be even more fruitful. . . . Remain in me,
and I will remain in you. No branch can bear fruit
by itself; it must remain in the vine. Neither can you
bear fruit unless you remain in me. I am the vine;
you are the branches. If a man remains in me and I
in him, he will bear much fruit; apart from me you
can do nothing. . . . If you remain in me and my
words remain in you, ask whatever you wish, and it
will be given you. . . . As the Father has loved me,
so have I loved you. Now remain in my love." (John
15:1-9)

Can you think of a better picture of oneness, of intimacy?
When God fills our daily focus—when we have the holy habit
of abiding in Him—He fills our being and is able to perform His
work through us.

But instead of keeping our focus on God, many of us have a
faulty focus. That was true of me for many years. I wanted my
life to "bear fruit," so I tried to imitate the lives of those believers whose walks with God I admired. Pretty soon, I was trying to
copy one person in one area and someone else in another area!
This never works! It is like a tree having an orange, some raspber-
ries, a pear, some grapes, strawberries, kiwi, and a dozen other
fruits all wired onto it. When God says He is going to bear fruit
through us, it's not fruit copied from someone else.

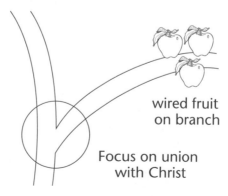

wired fruit
on branch

Focus on union
with Christ

God's fruit is His character: "But the fruit of the Spirit is love, joy, peace, patience, kindness, goodness, faithfulness, gentleness and self-control" (Galatians 5:22-23). When God works His fruit in you and in me, it will be unique. It will not be a copy of someone else.

When I returned to the United States after nine years in Ecuador, I was surprised that churches seemed to have their own culture. There was a "right" vocabulary, a "right" way to educate your children, and even "right" businesses to patronize! Many people in the church had a Christian doctor, plumber, mechanic, and shoe repairman. Somehow if a person chose to go to someone who was not a Christian, his or her relationship to God was suspect. It seemed that those choices had become a measure of a person's relationship with God! Such thinking perpetuates the lie that we are to be and look certain ways at the expense of a relationship that is dependent upon God to change us. God does not use a cookie cutter! Christlikeness is not behavior modification—changing how I behave in order to look good. God wants to make us holy, not simply good.

He wants to make us into new creatures—as new as when we were first born. Just as we were not able to do anything about our physical maturation, we are unable to do anything in the process of our becoming holy. We need God's divine breathing for our sanctification as well as for our salvation.

Becoming Holy

So how do we become holy? Stay connected to the vine. Jesus said, "Remain in me" (John 15:4). Some translations say "abide" or "live." The idea is to rest in Him.

Humanly, we find abiding or resting difficult, almost impossible. But the futility of doing anything more is made clear when we put the concept into modern terms. When I get on an airplane, I sit down in the seat. But what if I didn't put my entire weight in the seat for fear that the plane would not take off? Or worse yet, what if I spent the entire flight trying to help the plane make it to my destination? Would I make a difference? No. But I sure would have spent a lot of unnecessary energy. When we abide or rest, God does the work. If I am working so hard to try to get myself to where I think I need to be, I waste valuable strength and energy. When I "remain," I am connected to God and He will work *through* me. My prayer is "I will focus on *who* You are, and You take care of the fruit."

The result of clinging to the vine—having the holy habit of focusing on God—will be genuine fruit. That is transformation. It's not trying hard to produce, it is resting in God, hanging on to Him. Transformation begins with our hearts being captured by His character. When that happens, He will do the work. In 1 Peter 1:15, He gives us the command to be holy as He is, a seemingly impossible task, except that He has also said, "I am the LORD, who *makes* you holy" (Exodus 31:12, emphasis added). When He asks something of us, He provides the necessary tools with which to do it.

Hudson Taylor, the famous missionary to China, longed to be holy. He worked hard at it. He prayed, fasted, studied the Bible, carved out more time for prayer and meditation, and disciplined himself, all to no avail. He wrote,

> I knew if only I could abide in Christ all would be well, but I could not. . . . I thought that holiness, practical holiness, was to be gradually attained by diligent use of the means of grace. I felt that there was nothing I so much desired in the world . . . but the more I pursued . . . it, the more it eluded my grasp.[6]

Finally, through a letter from a coworker, Taylor was challenged to rest in God. As he studied the analogy of the vine and the branches in John 15, he recognized that the secret was not "asking how I am to get the sap out of the vine into myself, but remembering that Jesus is the vine. . . . Not seeking for faith to bring holiness but rejoicing in the fact of perfect holiness, in Christ. . . . Inseparably one with Him, this holiness is ours. His resources are mine, for He is mine. All this springs from the believer's oneness with Christ."[7]

This new insight turned Hudson Taylor's life upside down. He was freed from forcing himself to work and strive to be fruitful. His responsibility was to abide. God would take care of the rest.

Taylor called this the "exchanged life," a life lived by exchanging our physical, human efforts for the flow of His Spirit. As we focus on Him, it becomes easier to give Him the things that hinder His work in us. God takes from us those things that would kill and replaces them with that which would give us life. It is as if He takes a tumor of death out of us and replaces it with His wholeness.

Why is the exchanged life so hard for us to realize? Many times we don't allow ourselves to trust God. Since Adam and Eve, Satan has been successful at making humankind doubt God's trustworthiness. When we don't trust Him, we cannot release the old "stuff" that we hang on to. It is what we hang on to that keeps us from truly abiding in Him. God says, "Give it to me." I respond, "But Lord, I can't give it, that's *me!*" " I know," He says, "I want to transform you and make that part Me."

Many of us also spend too much time worrying about what we look like to other believers. We are concerned with what fruit we are producing, and we do not allow ourselves to become totally engaged with who God is and His desire to dwell within us absolutely. We obey God out of duty rather than love.

God created each one of us to be filled with Himself. He wants to transform us from within. The work that He does is absolutely magnificent. It is something we can take into eternity because it will be God Himself in us. If we abide in Him and dwell on Him, He will fill us. Then we will bear genuine fruit.

The Overflow of a Grateful Heart

As we rest with our focus on Him, He changes us from within. As He changes us, we become full. That is why in John 15:11, after Jesus teaches about abiding, He speaks of joy: "I have told you this so that my joy may be in you and that your joy may be complete." True abiding brings about joy (fruit). As He fills us with Himself, the joy of Christ dwelling within is like nothing on earth; you will find yourself spilling over with it.

That spilling over is called worship. Your heart becomes so full that you must burst into praise! "Oh, God, *You are so great!*" My favorite definition of worship is, "The overflow of a grateful heart under the sense of divine favor."[8] When we abide, we know His love. That is divine favor. Worship is the outpouring of a heart that knows God's love and presence. We have been made by God, bought by God, and then filled by Him. We are loved.

When we abide in Christ, we are not only free to worship, we *must* worship. God refers to His chosen ones as "the people I formed for myself that they may proclaim my praise" (Isaiah 43:21). Transformation frees us. When that happens, we can praise Him.

We read about another aspect of worship in Romans 12:1: "Therefore, I urge you, brothers, in view of God's mercy, to offer your bodies as living sacrifices, holy and pleasing to God—this is your spiritual act of worship." Total surrender to God is a "spiritual act of worship." Our response to His transformation brings about a change in the way we function. When our hearts overflow with gratitude and love to God, we will worship.

All we do can be an act of love and worship to God—even the normal responsibilities of life. Mundane, dull things are transformed into acts of adoration because we have been made free to worship. Even getting up with a sick child many times at night can become an act of love to God. During my years as a mother of little ones, my prayer was, "Father, you know that humanly speaking I'm absolutely spent, but I want to do this 'as unto You.'" Young mothers have told me, "I want to worship God but I don't have time. I'm just taking care of kids." Caring for our children can be an act of adoration to God. We can allow our love for God to come through us to our children and let them be the recipients of our worship.

Because my heart and body are the temple of the Lord, I can

worship God anytime, anywhere. Everything I do in this world, no matter how small or trivial, can be offered up to Him. "For such a man living itself will be sacramental and the whole world a sanctuary. His entire life will be priestly ministration. As he performs his never-so-simple task, he will hear the voice of the seraphim saying, 'Holy, Holy, Holy is the Lord of Hosts. The whole earth is full of His glory.'"[9]

In Matthew 25:40 Jesus says, "I tell you the truth, whatever you did for one of the least of these brothers of mine, you did for me." We can worship God all day long by saying, "I'm going to do this for You." "I'm going to take care of my husband to the best of my ability, out of my love for You." "I will care for my elderly mother as an act of worship before You." With that attitude, we fulfill the command, "So whether you eat or drink or whatever you do, do it all for the glory of God" (1 Corinthians 10:31). God can be the source of my love, and those around me become the objects of it.

When we choose to do things for other people as an act of worship, we are less concerned if they notice. I remember the first time I realized that my husband didn't recognize all the things I did for him. I was so disappointed. But God notices everything we do, no matter how small, if we do it as unto Him.

Angela told me about how she had eagerly volunteered to help a friend who had been seriously injured in a car accident. As the weeks went by, the responsibility of leaving her family daily and going to care for her friend began to weigh on her. Angela also felt that her friend, as helpless as she was, didn't seem to be as grateful for all her sacrifices of time and energy. Every day she went to her injured friend's house with less and less eagerness, and soon she became bitter about the hardships she was enduring to help her. One day in anger she said to God, "I can't do this anymore; get me out of this." But the Lord spoke to Angela's heart, "You have been looking to your friend for gratitude and appreciation, and you haven't been caring for her as unto Me." Everything changed when Angela's motivation became one of worship to Him!

Worship is a topic I have focused on for a good part of my life. I dedicated an entire year to studying it. In the first chapter of this book, I told about how I realized that I didn't know God well enough to worship Him. I had knowledge of God, but I had not cultivated a relationship with Him. As I learned to know God and abide in Him, He taught me how to worship Him. The Bible tells us that the Spirit will teach us all things. God is seeking those who will worship Him in spirit and truth (see John 4:23). "In spirit and in truth" means not just head knowledge, but truth. It means engaging my emotions—my spirit—so that I know Him well enough that all day long my heart can bubble up in worship because I am full of Him.

Power to Do What We Cannot

I appreciate how Richard Foster describes the transformation process: "The holiness tradition (the virtuous life) is concerned with the personal moral transformation that comes through the development of what the old writers called 'holy habits.' We are doing what we can (for example, engaging in the spiritual disciplines) in order to receive from God the power to do what we cannot (for example, loving our enemies). The one thread you will see . . . is the centrality of love as the motivation for holiness."[10]

God's love motivates us to develop holy habits to better focus on Him, and as a result of our focus, He works holiness in us.

Jerry Bridges also describes this process: "Growth in holiness, then, is not a matter of personal discipline plus God's work. It is a matter of dependent discipline, of recognizing that we are dependent on God to enable us to do what we are responsible to do. Then it is recognition that even when we have performed our duties, we must still look to Him to produce the growth."[11] First Corinthians 3:7 tells us, "So neither he who plants nor he who waters is anything, but only God, who makes things grow."

In the Face of His Kindness

When I started to understand what the Spirit of God wanted to do in me, I cried out in prayer, "My Lord, what can I do in the face of such kindness?" God reminded me of an incident from my childhood when boarding school was out and I was waiting for my family to pick me up and take me home. My black, metal trunk was packed and closed. All my classmates had waited months for this day to finally come. The older boys were placed as "scouts" high in the trees that lined the road to the boarding school. Each time a vehicle would come into sight, they called, "Here comes someone!" Even though I was playing, my heart was not in my play. Every time a car approached, my heart beat faster and I jumped up to see if it was my parents. Finally, after what seemed like forever, our dusty station wagon came into view. I couldn't stop grinning and ran over to get my younger brother. We both raced to the car before it stopped. My father had come to take us home.

I was going home for a new supply of kisses! When I had arrived in boarding school that year, I hadn't washed the side of my face where my parents had last kissed me until the dorm parent insisted I do so for health reasons. How happy I was to be going home! I, who was just another kid in the dorm, was going home where I was special. I, who was sick all the time with malaria, was going home to be pampered. I, who had no appetite and hated dorm food, was going home where my mother would fix tiny portions—just for me!

This trip home was going to be even more special because I had planned a surprise. Each term my parents gave us a dollar to spend on treats at the canteen. But out of love, I saved that dollar. For the previous three months, as the kids lined up to buy their goodies, I watched. While my peers ate their candy, I reveled in the anticipated joy of the gift I would give my mother. Not a dime had been spent; a whole dollar lay in my pocket.

On the way home my father stopped at the biggest town five hours from the mission station. I knew that there was a general store there that sold imported things. My heart beat with the thought of being able to purchase something special to take home to my mother. I mounted the steps to the store. To my dismay, the gifts from other countries were too expensive. Finally, I found a set of plastic salt and pepper shakers that fit my budget. The salt shaker was pink with a big "S" on it and the pepper shaker was blue with a large "P." It never occurred to me that I could only give because I had been given. I had no money of my own.

I will never forget my mother's reaction to my gift. Her eyes glowed with pleasure and her arms gathered me to her. The three months of hoarding and sacrifice were more than made up for by her response. She placed the pink and blue salt and pepper shakers in her china cabinet along with lovely pieces of china. She could not use the plastic shakers because of the high humidity in the jungle. Their presence among the china and crystal represented a child's ardent love.

Effects of Transformation

When our hearts overflow with love for God, we naturally look for ways to express the effects of the transforming work He does in our lives. You will not be able to contain the fullness of His work in your life, and you will burst with the desire to please God.

For example, I began looking for things I could do out of my ardent love for God. I looked at my home and would say, "Father, this is your home. Who would you have me use it for today?" Our home became a tool in my hand. I could use it as a platform from which I could express my love for God.

When we were in Ecuador, if we had leftovers I would put them on a plate with a fork and napkin and put it all in a bag. Then, I placed it on the outside wall of our house. I wanted the person who found it to feel value and worth and not eat my leftovers like a dog out of the trash. I would say, "My Lord, you know who is going up the street praying for tonight's meal. Help them find this and give You the glory."

Here in the United States we may not have homeless people walking past our homes, but we all have seen people standing on street corners with signs, "Will work for food," or asking for money. I carry a bag with a main meal in my car. It contains self-opening cans such as ravioli, fruit cocktail, and juice. I also include crackers, a fork, and a napkin. I store the bag behind the front seat within easy reach. I also keep an extra one in the trunk, so there is always something to give those who ask.

Many of us also have singles and elderly people in our lives. I have made a place in my freezer for single portions. After a big meal, I fill little containers with food. As I fix the *Once-A-Month* meals, I keep small containers available. One lasagna noodle bent back and forth on itself makes a wonderful portion for an older person. I buy a little extra and have this section of my freezer full and ready for distribution. My prayer as I fill this designated corner of my freezer is "Lord, these things are here for You to use. My hands are Yours to help whoever You would want." There is one elderly woman I visit regularly with a week's supply of meals for her freezer. I've been known to carry a bag of frozen meals to church to hand to a busy single. We invite hungry students to our home and I often try to send something home with them. When I hear of a need, my freezer has a supply that can help meet that need.

The more I focus on God, the more I want to worship Him. Because I want to give God the "first fruits" of my week, every Monday I look over the week's schedule and choose one morning to dedicate to worship. Then in preparation for that time, I select music that aids me in focusing on His character. I love Handel's *Messiah*; it shows the plan of God for the ages. I use a lot of music in my worship, for it allows me to express thoughts that cannot be expressed in words.

In the beginning, I always worshiped in the same place. I found that if I changed places, the dust under the cupboard or the child's ball that I saw peeking out from under the dresser distracted me. I sometimes worship with a Walkman. For each time of worship, I tell my Lord that I want to make a special appointment with the God Most High. I do not answer the phone during that time because I have another engagement. This is our time together. I love fulfilling what God wanted when He said, "I will be their God and they will be my people" (Jeremiah 31:33).

Now that our children are grown, I try to spend time in

worship during the afternoon before dinner. This, I tell my Lord, is to make sure that there is enough praise going up before His throne. I often tell Him that many of my brothers and sisters cannot spend that time in quietness before Him because of their family and schedule demands, but I am here on their behalf.

As I drop off to sleep I ask the Lord to awaken the family of God on the other side of the world, as their day is dawning, and give them a new song to sing to the Lord.

I previously mentioned a verse in Isaiah that changed the way I worship. I saw the heart of God in this verse. God says that believers are "the people I formed for myself that they may proclaim my praise. Yet you have not called upon me, O Jacob, you have not wearied yourselves for me, O Israel. You have not brought me sheep for burnt offerings, nor honored me with your sacrifices. I have not burdened you with grain offerings nor wearied you with demands for incense. You have not bought any fragrant calamus for me, or lavished on me the fat of your sacrifices" (Isaiah 43:21-24).

The Israelites weren't giving their best to God. They had lost the understanding of the privilege they had to worship where His glory dwelt. The fat of the sacrifice meant that the lamb had been cared for and reared with the express purpose of taking him to God in an act of worship. Calamus was a special ingredient that was used to make the incense for the temple. It was costly and rare. The burning of this unique incense represented extravagant worship. It took exceptional effort to obtain the spice and often meant a trip to a foreign country. God knew that without calamus, the people's worship was a ritual without love or heart commitment.

For the Israelites, worship had become a ritual to do and be done with. The Isaiah passage challenged me to think of all the things I could do to show God that I had lavished my best on Him. I searched throughout my heart for the calamus of my life. My prayer many times is, "Father, show me how I can best give of myself today so that You will know that I honor You in the secret place of my heart."

Today my worship looks different than it used to. I spill over with joy and fullness from deep within my soul because I am filled with God's love and presence. God orchestrates my worship, as my heart becomes an instrument of praise that the Holy Spirit plays to the Father and the Son. Most of the time no one knows worship is going on in the temple of my heart. I may be in the checkout line at the grocery story, at a dinner party, or watching the evening news. On one level I am fully engaged with what is going on around me, but on another, I sing His praises from deep within my soul.

> So we have the activity of the everlasting Trinity focused around our frail prayers. God the Spirit is interpreting our sighs and groans before the throne of heaven. God the Son is interceding on our behalf before the throne. And God the Father, who sits on the throne of heaven, is using our prayers to form a perfect soliloquy—God speaking to God.[12]

When we enter into the new covenant with God, we are His people. As His people we can abide in Him. We do not need to strive to pray, to worship, or to produce. He does that when we look to Him.

P R A Y E R

Oh my Father,
I am in such need of Your work in my life.
I need faith to believe that "what
You have begun, You will do."
Help me to have a heart that is easily
molded into Your image.
You taught me to say, "Thy will be done," but I want more.
I want Your will to be the very passion
and drive of my being.
Help me, Lord.
Amen.

STUDY AND DISCUSSION QUESTIONS

1. We are not the only ones who like to copy Christians that we know. Read 1 Corinthians 3:1-9 to see how Paul responded to the early church regarding the trouble of copying man. How does Paul diagnose the problem?

2. Read 2 Corinthians 3:3. What does it tell us about how God writes on our hearts? Meditate on the significance of the name "living God." What does that say to you?

3. What do Romans 12:2 and Ephesians 4:23-24 tell us about how transformation comes about? What is the end result of transformation according to the Ephesians 4 passage? What does it mean to you in light of the importance of where your focus is?

4. Read 2 Corinthians 3:18. What do we reflect? What are we being transformed into? With what are we being transformed? Who is the source of it? Describe how this verse works itself out in your life.

5. What does 1 Thessalonians 4:1-9 tell us about why it is God's will that we are sanctified?

6. Many of us might have thought that the spiritual work done in our lives begins and ends with salvation. Read the truth of Philippians 1:6,9-11. What are Paul's requests to God for the Philippians? What is the "good work" Paul is talking about here? Where does he say the fruit comes from?

7. According to Romans 6:19, "slavery to righteousness" leads to what? In light of what we've said in this chapter, what do you think slavery to righteousness consists of? (See Romans 6:22 for additional insight.)

8. What is the hope of a heart that is being transformed according to 1 John 3:1-3?

9. Read Romans 12:1. The first point is God's mercy, which is a part of His love. What does Paul ask us to do in view of God's mercy and love? What kind of sacrifice does He want, and how does God view that? How would we fulfill this verse in light of the definition, "Worship is the overflow of a grateful heart under the sense of divine favor"?

10. Use the following verse from the hymn by F. R. Havergal as a model for your own prayer. Offer each part of your body up as a gift of love to God.

Take my hands and let them move

At the impulse of Thy love,

Take my feet, and let them be

Swift and "beautiful" for Thee.

$\mathcal{D}$aily $\mathcal{W}$isdom

Transformation of the Mind

$\mathcal{A}$LBERT WAS A WISE, ELDERLY MAN WHO SERVED AS A DEACON in a large, traditional church across the street from a state university. The church had been casting about for ways to reach the large population of students living practically next door. They had not come up with anything. One Sunday after the service began and the pews were full, the doors opened. In walked a young man, obviously a student from the school across the street. He was barefoot, his dirty hair flowed down his back, and he was wearing a tattered T-shirt and jeans. Obviously, he didn't know how to dress for church!

The congregation watched surreptitiously as he searched for a seat. Finally after getting almost to the front of the church, he squatted in the center aisle on the carpet. A feeling of discomfort ran through the crowd. They couldn't let him sit there on the floor—after all, he wasn't dressed right and the sight of him was distracting. Soon, Albert came from the back of the church. His white head bobbed as he slowly and carefully tapped his way down the aisle with his cane. He made a striking figure in his three-piece suit and pocket watch. He was godly, elegant, and dignified. Nobody envied him the job that he was about to do, but someone had to do it. All activity stopped and the sanctuary became utterly silent as the church watched Albert make his way to the young student. The preacher couldn't even preach his sermon until the deacon did what he had to do.

The congregation watched smugly as Albert dropped his cane to the floor and sat down beside the young man. When it became clear that Albert had no intention of reprimanding the man, but instead was planning to sit beside him during the service, the people choked up with emotion. The pastor stood and, when he gained control, said, "What I say you will never remember, but what you have seen today, you will never forget."[1]

The wisdom that comes from God is unlike any other wisdom: "But the wisdom that comes from heaven is first of all pure; then peace-loving, considerate, submissive, full of mercy and good fruit, impartial and sincere" (James 3:17). God's wisdom can be sitting down beside someone in silence. Wisdom can be pulling back the covers of a bed for a weary mother, an exhausted executive, or a drained wife who needs rest. Wisdom can be wiping away tears without saying a word, or feeding someone with a broken heart. When someone is in grief and has a swollen throat from suppressing tears, a bowl of soup or something easy to swallow can go a long way toward ministering to a heart that hurts.

The Traits of Godly Wisdom

For years I believed that such wisdom came with age; that is why I faithfully went to nursing homes to collect the wisdom of the elderly. I learned that not all elderly people are wise, nor is intelligence a prerequisite for wisdom. Even an ungodly person can be considered wise.

Since the beginning of time, people from all scholarly

disciplines, cultures, and social strata have recognized wisdom. For example:

- Antisthenes, a Greek philosopher who lived from 444—365 B.C., said, "That learning is most requisite which unlearns evil."[2] He had observed the world around him and concluded, wisely, the value of "unlearning" evil.
- Buddha also had many sage observations about life. He said, "Hatred does not cease by hatred, but only by love; this is the eternal rule."[3]
- Nobel Prize winning physicist Arthur H. Compton stated, "Every great discovery I ever made, I gambled that the truth was there, then I acted on it in faith until I could prove its existence."[4]
- Immanuel Kant said, "Two things fill me with constantly increasing admiration and awe, the longer and more earnestly I reflect on them: a starry heaven without and a moral law within."[5]

This is worldly wisdom. The person with worldly wisdom is a truth seeker who acquires knowledge and credentials. She is a moral person who may live by God's truth, but does not recognize God as the Author of truth. She worships the creation but not the Creator. Worldly wisdom can be "collected."

Godly wisdom, on the other hand, comes from our relationship with God. First Corinthians 1:30 tells us about "Christ Jesus who has become for us wisdom from God." The woman with godly wisdom seeks to *know* God and to become like Him. As she becomes like Him, He graces her with godly wisdom—His wisdom—and her life brings God glory. "To walk along this way, to journey toward this place of wisdom, is to waken to the presence of the risen Christ. It is to risk discovering the mystery of God alive at the very center of one's being."[6] We cannot walk with an intellectual concept, we have to walk with a person. "[The labyrinth journey] becomes a metaphor for evoking the gradual discovery of God's intimate presence."[7] Knowing about Jesus will not satisfy our need for divine wisdom. Only a relationship with Him cultivates godly wisdom within us.

When God is our daily focus, He infuses us with His wisdom. Godly wisdom, the byproduct of knowing God, builds character. Dr. Joseph Stowell of Moody Bible Institute wrote concerning the difference between just knowing *about* God and actually *knowing* God:

> It is time that we who are committed to authentic Christianity value character over credentials. Credentials are transient; character is permanent; credentials build memories about what we have done; character builds a legacy for others to follow. Credentials are locked in one person; character is transferable. Credentials will get us in the front door; character will keep us there. Credentials tend to evoke jealousy; character attracts respect and stimulates others to develop character as well.[8]

We could paraphrase his statement this way: "Knowledge is transient; wisdom is permanent; knowledge builds memories about what we have done; wisdom builds a legacy for others to follow. Knowledge is locked in one person; wisdom is transferable. Knowledge will get us in the front door; wisdom will keep us there. Knowledge tends to evoke jealousy; wisdom attracts respect and stimulates others to develop wisdom as well." Credentials and knowledge are earned and can be the source of pride. But godly wisdom comes from God—we know it is not of us.

When we have acquired a lot of information *about* God but do not have a vibrant, moment-by-moment relationship *with* Him, our "wisdom" rings hollow. I was reminded of this recently when a friend excitedly told me about a book she was reading. Later, she called to say that she had been invited for dinner with the author. She had read the book and was eager to meet the person responsible for it. She had expected the author to be gentle and godly, full of grace and wisdom. What she found, instead, was a bitter, withdrawn woman who did not reflect what she had written. This author had written a book of facts *about* God, but her words did not flow from an intimate relationship *with* God. She had knowledge, but she was not depending on the Source of wisdom.

Many people make this same mistake. Take the apostle Paul, for example. As a Pharisee, Paul had all the training, schooling, and knowledge that a person of his day could have. He studied under Gamaliel, a well-known and respected teacher. Not only that, his father had been a Pharisee before him, so Paul had been taught about God from childhood. He stated in Acts 26:5 that he had managed to keep the Law, which was no small feat. But his life was turned upside down when he encountered the Living Wisdom and committed himself to Him. Paul's relationship with the Living Wisdom changed his heart. Today his letters are studied and scrutinized because he walked with God and became wise. He wrote:

> Where is the wise man? Where is the scholar? Where is the philosopher of this age? Has not God made foolish the wisdom of the world? For since in the wisdom of God the world through its wisdom did not know him, . . . My message and my preaching were not with wise and persuasive words, but with a demonstration of the Spirit's power, so that your faith might not rest on men's wisdom, but on God's power. We do, however, speak a message of wisdom among the mature, but not the wisdom of this age or of the rulers of this age, who are coming to nothing. No, we speak of God's secret wisdom, a wisdom that has been hidden and that God destined for our glory before time began. (1 Corinthians 1:20-21, 2:4-7)

God's "secret wisdom" comes with no diploma; we do not graduate from the school of godly wisdom. It is a lifelong process.

Guided by God's Wise Voice

God is "the only wise God" (Romans 16:27). His wisdom is part of His essence. A.W. Tozer defines God's wisdom this way: "It sees the end from the beginning, so there can be no need to guess or conjecture. Wisdom sees everything in focus each in proper relation to all. . . ."[9] He knows everything in the detail that only an eternal, all-powerful being can. J. I. Packer says, "Wisdom is . . . found in its fullness only in God. He alone is naturally, entirely, and invariably wise."[10]

God's wisdom is in us in the person of the living Christ. He walks with us and wants to talk with us. If we choose to tune our hearts to His voice, we can hear Him. He whispers wisdom to us because He embodies all that it is: "Those who obey his commands live in him, and he in them. And this is how we know that he lives in us: We know it by the Spirit he gave us" (1 John 3:24). We have living wisdom dwelling with us! Not only does Christ embody wisdom, He is the way to it.

Paul tells us, "Let the word of Christ dwell in you richly as you teach and admonish one another with all wisdom" (Colossians 3:16). In other words, the written and living Word can occupy, capture, and fill us. God's Word is to take up residence in us, filling every part of us. As His Spirit lives within us and we respond to Him, He helps us understand His Word. Through Jesus' extravagant, generous occupancy, He unbars our hearts to the treasure of Scripture.

I've found that the best way for me to "dwell richly" in God's Word is to take a year to study a particular topic. "It is far better to find a few spiritual staples and feed on them until they mold you."[11] I've studied the character of God, the attributes of God, wisdom, and holiness, among other things. My friend Connie spent two years studying Proverbs every day in her quiet time. Her life has been profoundly affected by her detailed, intimate understanding of those passages. Her approach to her children and home life has been changed as she has sought to apply the principles of the book of Proverbs.

As you read and study God's Word, ask God to give you wisdom about what it means and how to apply it to your life *today*. In Acts 8:26-40, God sent Philip from Samaria to a desert road to explain the Scriptures to an Ethiopian man who desired to worship and know God's Word. God was very specific with Philip, saying, "Go south to the road—the desert road—that goes down from Jerusalem to Gaza" (verse 26). When he got there, God said, "Go to that chariot and stay near it" (verse 29). There he found the Ethiopian man reading the Scriptures as he traveled. Philip climbed into the chariot and helped him understand what he was reading. Later, Philip baptized the man before they went their separate ways. Just as God met the Ethiopian eunuch's need for understanding, He will do the same for us through the Holy Spirit.

When I am studying Scripture or preparing to speak and come across a passage that I don't understand, I stop and pray for specific insight into God's purpose in those verses. I consult commentaries and students of God's Word. Most often, however, the insight comes as I sit in prayer before the heavenly Father. *He is alive in us.* When we cultivate sensitivity to the voice of living wisdom in us, we will learn understanding.

How do we know when we hear God's voice? Jesus said, "I am the good shepherd; I know my sheep and my sheep know me" (John 10:14). He also said that the shepherd calls to the sheep and "his sheep follow him because they know his voice" (John 10:4). When we cultivate a sensitivity to His voice, we learn to hear it. The more aware we are of His speaking, the more often we will hear Him. People use different terms to describe how they know that God has spoken; they say they "sensed" His voice, or something was "impressed" upon them, or they "felt" God's direction. To hear God's voice involves an element of faith on the part of the hearer as well as an openness to His speaking.

God's voice is often very specific, especially when He points out sin in our lives. For example, when He convicts me about something I have said, usually He reminds me of the incident, the person, and the words I said: "Your comment on Wednesday night to Suzie about her neighbor was hurtful and wrong."

But what if I'm not sure that what I've heard comes from God? We should always line up what we hear or feel God is saying to us with the truth of the Word of God. God will *never* tell us something contrary to the truth found in His Word.

When we hear God's voice, the truth of what He says pierces the heart. If what you believe God is saying to you finds a strong response of affirmation (either for conviction of sin or for a positive direction), then you can check it with the truth of the Scriptures to confirm the rightness of it.

God will teach you if you listen to Him, and He can speak through means other than Scripture. Watch for His Spirit communicating with you through the voice of a child, a song, a soft breeze, or a ray of sunshine. His fingerprints are everywhere if we will choose to recognize them. He will use His Word, the input of others, circumstances, and many other things unusual to one whose heart is not attuned to Him. Everything that is important to us is important to Him. We will hear His whisper of guidance as we seek His wisdom on matters of daily living, but often His guidance is given only as we need it and not before. Let me illustrate.

My tiny grandmother and I were walking in the dark jungle. Grandma was carrying a lantern that gave out very little light. We were talking happily when I realized that I could not see anything ahead. I panicked. The darkness closed in around me and the night sounds were terrifying. I froze. Grandma turned and asked me what the problem was. I told her that I was too frightened to go on. I was afraid of what I didn't know . . . of what was ahead in the darkness.

Grandma set the lantern on the ground and asked if there was anything I could see in the light that was frightening. I studied the circle that the lamp cast and concluded all was well within it. I assured her that what I could see was fine; it was what I could not see that scared me. She took a few steps further down the path, drawing me with her because of my fear of being left in the dark. Once again, she put the lamp down on the ground. "Are you frightened by what you see here?" she asked. "No," I answered slowly, as her point began to dawn on me.

Grandma went on to say that God is like that. He will walk with us and give us all the light we need for the next step. Every time we move forward, He will light the way, but the future remains in His hands, covered until we get there.

Because we confuse godly wisdom with earthly wisdom, it is easy to want to try to borrow ahead for future possibilities and worries. For example:

- What will you ever do if your children do not turn out well? God will be there.
- What will happen if your husband leaves you for another woman? God will be there.
- What would you do if your child was killed? God will be there.

He does not give us wisdom ahead of time because He will be right there with you, whispering His response to your uncertainties and fears.

Rest in Who God Is

Tozer says, "We rest in what God is."[12] God's wisdom aids us in dealing with the nitty gritty of life, right where we live!

Rosa was an Ecuadorian woman who helped me run our home during the nine years we lived on the equator. Each market day would find me reading the shopping list to her. I could not understand why she would need to have it read out loud, unless I had explained it poorly. One day I realized that my communication skills were not the problem—Rosa could not read. Rosa knew God, and the wisdom that He taught her was her guiding light instead of knowledge gained from education. As she worked around my home, I could hear her breathing her prayers to God, "O mi Señor," checking in with Him constantly. An uneducated woman looking to her God for wisdom, Rosa is an example to me. She had no formal training, yet she was one of the wisest women I knew. One day she found a mother sobbing on the street. "Will you please help me? My two teenage daughters have been missing for months and I am desperate to find them." Rosa took that encounter as an assignment from God. She first checked all the hospitals and morgues to rule out the possibility of their deaths, praying all the time for guidance. Then one day someone suggested she try an area of town that was known for drug users.

She was warned not to go alone, but she said, "My God is with me; if He can't protect me, nobody can!" She picked her way through the muddy roads littered with young people, some sitting, others lying on the ground, all with glazed eyes. Some of the young men threatened her, but she stood her ground and asked, once again, of the whereabouts of the two sisters. Various clues led to her finding the girls living in a filthy corner of a room with eight to ten other addicted kids. Rosa spoke to everyone in the room of God's love and challenged them to get out of the vicious circle they lived in. As the girls gathered the few belongings they had, several other teenagers broke into tears and asked her to take them home too. When Rosa left that dangerous area, she had four young people in tow. She restored them to their families and challenged each one with accepting Christ as their personal Savior. God gave Rosa the love and wisdom to accomplish what city authorities and others had tried to do for years.

Godly wisdom is planted in our hearts by His loving residence as we seek to know Him better. It is the flowering of our preoccupation with God and who He is. When we look to Him, He gives wisdom one day at a time. We can rest in God and free Him to work His wisdom in us daily.

PRAYER

Oh, the depths of the riches of the
wisdom and knowledge of God!
How unsearchable his judgments,
and his paths beyond tracing out!
"Who has known the mind of the Lord?
Or who has been his
counselor? Who has ever given to God,
that God should repay him?"
For from him and through him and to him are all things.
To him be the glory forever!
Amen.
(Romans 11:33-36)

STUDY AND DISCUSSION QUESTIONS

1. Job 28:28, Psalm 111:10, Proverbs 1:7, and Proverbs 9:10 all speak of the "fear of the Lord" and wisdom. If the "fear of the Lord" means to recognize His power and His presence, how is it godly wisdom?

2. According to 1 Corinthians 1:30, who or what is wisdom from God? What else comes with it?

3. First Corinthians 2:6-16 speaks about where wisdom comes from and the purpose of it. Make notes about the significant aspects of wisdom mentioned in this passage.

4. The Bible speaks of the gaining of wisdom as a journey. Read Proverbs 2:6-11, Proverbs 4:11-15, and Hosea 14.

   a. What do these passages tell us about what wisdom is?

   b. What do they tell us about what it is not?

   c. How do they describe the way of wisdom?

5. Proverbs 2:3-6, Ecclesiastes 2:26, Daniel 2:21, Luke 21:15, and James 1:5 all contain promises of wisdom. Read the verses and answer the following questions for each one.

    a. What else besides wisdom does God promise?

    b. What prerequisites (if any) are there in order to be eligible for the promise?

6. Read the definition of godly wisdom in James 3:17 and compare it with the list of the fruit of the Spirit in Galatians 5:22-23. Based on what we know of how the fruit of the Spirit is developed in our lives, explain how the characteristics of wisdom can be developed in the life of a believer. Write a paraphrase or your own statement about the importance of wisdom.

7. How have you seen the difference between knowledge and wisdom played out in your own life? How have you seen it in others?

CHAPTER ELEVEN

Daily Contentment

Transformation of the Heart

YEARS AGO I TRAVELED TO A NURSING HOME TO VISIT MY father's mother and her sister. Grandma had her large hat pulled low over her eyes to protect them from the light. She kept her eyes closed "to save her eyesight." Auntie Teeto was bent and bowed. Grandma had enjoyed a life of relative comfort while Auntie Teeto's was one of difficulty. Although they were sisters, the two women had little resemblance to each other. They came from the same family, had the same background, and now were living in the same place, but they had opposite reactions to everything around them.

When I arrived, they showed me around the place they called home. Auntie Teeto turned and said to me, "Isn't it wonderful how clean the place is? The floors are so shiny!" Grandma remarked, "The floors are too slippery—you can't walk on them! We'll break our necks!"

The bell rang for dinner, and we moved to the dining room where dinner was served. After prayer, we were served a plate with pork chops, potatoes, and vegetables. Auntie Teeto began the conversation. "Isn't it wonderful that we don't have to cook?" Wrestling with her pork chop, Grandma complained, "This is the toughest thing I've ever tasted."

After supper we moved to a small reception area. The nursing home was next door to a skating rink, and as darkness closed in on the neighborhood, the noise from the rink became louder. Grandma was disgusted. "This place is so noisy, there's never any peace and quiet. You can hardly hear yourself think!" Auntie Teeto looked at me with a twinkle in her eye and said, "Isn't it wonderful that we have ears to hear all that is going on around us!"

Two sisters and two choices. One was a woman of contentment and the other a woman of complaint. It was a pleasure to visit with Auntie Teeto and just as much a chore to spend time with my grandmother. I knew what kind of woman I wanted to become.

A Change in Perspective

Contentment does not come through changed circumstances; it comes through a transformation of the heart. If we practice the holy habit of focusing on God, we come to see Him as the Giver of all good gifts. As God does His work of transformation within us, He can help us to see even the simple things in life as gifts from Him. Slowly the heart becomes satisfied with God alone.

God fills us with Himself and begins a work to bring out the best in us because He is making something new. He is making you, with all that you lack, with all your weaknesses, into a new person. Paul said to the Galatians, "I am again in the pains of childbirth until Christ is formed in you" (4:19). This transforming work that God does in our hearts is not the best of earth, but the very best of heaven, for it is our blessed Lord who is shining His character through us.

The apostle Paul wrote, "I am not saying this because I am in need, for I have learned to be content whatever the circumstances. I know what it is to be in need, and I know what it is to have plenty. I have learned the secret of being content in any and every situation, whether well fed or hungry, whether living in plenty or in want. I can do everything through him who gives me strength" (Philippians 4:11-13). God gives us the will and the strength to be content.

When Paul wrote this passage, stoicism was a prevalent philosophy. Like the Christians of the day, stoics sought contentment, but they defined it as "a frame of mind which was completely independent of all outward things, and which carried the secret of happiness within itself."[1] Bible scholar William Barclay wrote:

> The Stoic said, "I will learn contentment by a deliberate act of my own will." Paul said, "I can do all things through Christ who infuses his strength into me." For the Stoic, contentment was a human achievement; for Paul, it was a divine gift. The Stoic was *self-sufficient*; but Paul was *God-sufficient*. Stoicism failed because it was inhuman; Christianity succeeded because it was rooted in the divine.[2]

As I mentioned in the beginning of this book, I used to think contentment was something I could will myself into feeling. But like the Stoics, I was putting my trust in self rather than in God. It's an easy trap to fall into. I have a friend who has one of the strongest wills I've ever known. She told me her strong will, which is a positive force in much of what she does, is a hindrance in her walk with God. For years she tried to "will" herself to be godly. But through pain and rejection, she discovered that it wasn't until she yielded her will to God's Holy Spirit that He was free to work in her. It was only after her submission to God that she began to see evidence of godliness in her life. Her will got in the way of God's freedom to make her more like Him.

Contentment is a fruit, or work, that God does in us when our hearts are fully engaged with Him. It is something that starts inside and works itself out. What enables us to be content regardless of what's going on around us? The bedrock assurance of God's presence. Hebrews 13:5 says, "Keep your lives free from the love of money and be content with what you have, because God has said, 'Never will I leave you; never will I forsake you.'" In other words, when we are preoccupied with Him and His presence, He works contentment in our hearts. You and I can know beyond the shadow of a doubt that He is with us, and that He is sovereign over what we do and do not have.

David prayed: "Show me your ways, O LORD, teach me your paths; guide me in your truth and teach me" (Psalm 25:4-5). I believe this prayer pleases God. Without the Spirit's help, we cannot gain godly contentment. Our God has promised, "I will put my Spirit in you and move you to follow my decrees and be careful to keep my laws" (Ezekiel 36:27). He wants us to obey Him, and He helps us to do that because our obedience pleases Him. When we begin to respond to the teaching of the Spirit, contentment slowly follows.

This contentment is independent of outward circumstances. Barclay refers to it as the "Christian disentanglement of heart,"[3] and Paul writes:

> For we brought nothing into the world, and we can take nothing out of it. But if we have food and clothing, we will be content with that. People who want to get rich fall into temptation and a trap and into many foolish and harmful desires that plunge men into ruin and destruction. For the love of money is a root of all kinds of evil. Some people, eager for money, have wandered from the faith and pierced themselves with many griefs. (1 Timothy 6:7-10)

The Holy Spirit can help us to disentangle our hearts from our circumstances when we yield ourselves to His teaching. Honduran-born Alexandra was a teenager when both her parents died. The only legacy she had from them were some lovely pieces of furniture. When God called her and her husband to go to Costa Rica as missionaries, Alexandra learned she could not take her parents' furniture with her. She would have to sell it. It broke her heart to separate herself from all that she had left of her parents. At first she refused, but finally after weeks of wrestling, she yielded herself to what God asked of her.

She told me of the freedom she experienced once she had placed her possessions into God's hands. I was sitting in her living room in Costa Rica as we talked. The simple decorations and furniture made it clear that she and her husband could not buy even the basics. But I could not keep my eyes off Alexandra's radiant face as she talked about how God had met her. Here was a woman who had transferred her affections from her possessions to God. She knew contentment apart from her circumstances and had found Him to be more than she needed.

Please realize that I'm *not* encouraging you to deny the hard things in life. For our emotional health, we have to acknowledge the hardships that we deal with, but we do not have to dwell on them. When we focus on the difficult things in our lives, it is easy to complain. However, we can choose to recognize the hard things but concentrate on the good things.

For example, if I am planning to make a fruit salad with apples and I discover I have no apples, I can do one of several things. I can be very upset and do nothing, or I can make a fruit salad with the other fruit I do have. Or, as the old saying goes, "When life serves you lemons, make lemonade!"

Like Paul, we can focus on God and see His hand and perspective even in the difficult things. When we gripe and complain we are grumbling against the very One who has provided for us—the God of the universe who loves us and can motivate us to reject outright those negative thoughts. Ask God to hold captive your contrary and complaining thoughts. Then when thoughts do come, one at a time, take them to the "pen" where He is holding all those thoughts. Pray that God will make you aware when you are tempted to complain and ask that He would give you His perspective instead. Remember that you are turning from one thing to another.

This is often very difficult, as you are part of generations who have committed the sin of an unthankful heart. This is one of the most insidious sins that is passed down "to the third and fourth generation" (Exodus 34:7). The warning label for this part of your walk says, "Caution! You will not be able to do this by yourself. You need a Mighty God."

When I was a child, my parents taught me to look into the face of the giver of a gift and say "thank you." We can look up from the gift to the hand of the giver and learn what's in his or her heart. God's gifts tell us that He is without limit in His power, He sustains all things by His Spirit forever, He made us, and He is sustaining us for eternity. He is faithful. He loves us. We can count on Him. We don't go to God and find Him in a bad mood. He is always the same. He is complete.

I have a notebook entitled, "My Book of Remembrance." In it I have recorded the simple gifts of God that I often take for granted. I began with things that I had not thanked God for in a long time: my hair, my skin, the ability to move without pain, a roof over my head, and so on. I wrote down as many things as God brought to mind. Any time something good happened, I wrote it down as evidence of God's hand in my life. It became a record of gratitude and a wonderful tool to teach our children how to thank God for what He does and who He is.

When we have a record of how He has taken care of us, it builds our faith and strengthens our ability to rest in His capacity to take care of our circumstances. The result? Contentment! God has given us so much, and we have so little we can give back. A thankful, contented heart is a gift we give to Him. This is a win/win situation. God fills your heart with Himself and then lets you give that full gift back to Him. Then you are blessed for "your" gift. God says, "Wherever I cause my name to be honored, I will come to you and bless you" (Exodus 20:24).

Come Full Circle

I have said that contentment comes when we have the holy habit of focusing on God. But there is a byproduct that I never anticipated at the beginning of this journey of knowing God and becoming like Him. As I have cultivated a contented heart, my heart has slowly been transformed and turned more fully toward Him. As I became less concerned over whether I had certain things or whether the situations in my life were good, I was freer to engage with God Himself. His active presence in my life called me to godliness.

Paul reinforced that truth when he challenged Timothy: "But godliness with contentment is great gain" (1 Timothy 6:6). The greatest gain for me was the new closeness to God that I experienced as I learned to choose to be content with what He had given me. Contentment plugged the hole in my heart, allowing me to focus on the Giver rather than scrambling for the gifts that I was not even enjoying!

A Woman of Contentment

I would like to leave you with one last picture of contentment.

At the end of her life, my mother suffered from Alzheimer's. She was in a nursing home and often did not recognize me. Mother shared her room with another woman about the same age. Her roommate was sloppy and often left things strewn everywhere. My mother had been an immaculate housekeeper, and even though she didn't know what day it was, she continued to carefully maintain order. One afternoon I helped her get to the bathroom so she could wash her hands. She stood at the sink and surveyed the dirt and chaos left by her roommate. An expression of disgust came over her face and she began to complain. But just as quickly she stopped herself and I heard her say, "But that would not please my Lord!"

For weeks I grieved that I was not able to talk with her to find out how she had learned contentment. After her death, I sorted through her things. In a pile of books, I found a small, old, loose-leaf notebook with hand-lettered dividers. My heart stopped as I opened the little book and discovered thoughts and notes that my mother had written over the years.

One page jumped out at me. Copied in her careful lettering from a favorite book, it was titled, "If we wish to gain contentment we might try these rules":

- Allow ourselves to complain of nothing, not even the weather.
- Never picture ourselves in any circumstances in which we are not.
- Never compare our lot with that of another.
- Never allow ourselves to wish that this or that had been otherwise.
- Never dwell on the morrow; remember that is God's and not ours.[4]

With awe, I knelt to thank God for His gift of insight.

When our minds are gone, what will we have to offer God? If we have cultivated contentment, we can offer that to Him even when we cannot control what we think. We choose contentment today in order for it to be ours forever.

PRAYER

Lord, I want to draw near, as a child
who snuggles close in the lap of a parent.
I want to let Your presence fill me so that I am full of You.
Help me, oh my Father, to let
Your Spirit teach me contentment
so that I am not distracted by my lack of "things"
and forget that You want to satisfy
my longing heart with the eternal.
Amen.

S T U D Y   A N D   D I S C U S S I O N
Q U E S T I O N S

1. What do you learn about the teaching of the Holy Spirit from Psalm 25:9, Luke 12:12, and 1 John 2:27?

2. Read John 4:10, Acts 2:38, Romans 6:23, and James 1:17. Make a note of what gift from God is referred to in each passage. Make a list of some other things that you experience in your own life as gifts from God.

3. Read Numbers 14:26-29. The Israelites were complaining about their situation, but three times God tells Moses and Aaron what really was at the root of their complaints. What was that? What were the consequences of their attitude? Read Numbers 14:24. What made the difference in Caleb? What did he receive as a result of that?

4. Read Proverbs 30:7-9. What is Solomon's prayer? Why does he ask that? How do these verses relate to choosing contentment as a mind-set?

5. Read Jesus' words in Luke 3:14. How can you put the words of Jesus into practice in your life?

6. How can God's promise in 2 Corinthians 9:8 help you to choose contentment?

7. Read Romans 1:21. What was the end result for those who knew God but did not glorify Him or give thanks? Explain how you think this could happen.

8. Proverbs 15:15 and Proverbs 17:1-2 mention only a few of the benefits of contentment. What other benefits can you think of?

9. Each of the five things in my mother's notebook is supported in Scripture. Read them again and answer the questions that follow.

- Allow ourselves to complain of nothing, not even the weather. (Philippians 2:14, 1 Corinthians 10:10)
- Never picture ourselves in any circumstances in which we are not. (Philippians 4:11-13)
- Never compare our lot with that of another. (2 Corinthians 10:12, Psalm 84:10-11)
- Never allow ourselves to wish that this or that had been otherwise. (Romans 8:28)
- Never dwell on the morrow; remember that is God's and not ours. (Matthew 6:25-34, Philippians 4:6-7)

a. Which one of the statements hits you the hardest? Why? Look up the verse that applies to the statement and write a short paragraph explaining how you can implement that in your own life.

b. Choose another one of the statements that might be an area of difficulty for you. Add any other verses you can think of that support the statement. Then write a prayer asking God to help you specifically in that area.

CHAPTER TWELVE

Walking with the Eternal One

Transformation of the Soul

I WAS GLAD THE CHILDREN WERE QUIET FOR THE TRIP HOME AFTER church. I was in no mood for chatter. My spirit was in turmoil. I felt there was a discrepancy between the way my life was and the way I felt it should be. I could easily think about God and lofty spiritual concepts on Sunday when the children were in the nursery and the only demand on my attention was a wonderful church service. But the way I lived the rest of the week really revealed what was going on in my soul: my life was compartmentalized.

I mentioned previously that my parents and grandparents had spent most of their adult lives as missionaries in Africa. I looked at their life work and felt it amounted to much more for eternity than mine. All I was doing was carpooling, laundry, cooking, washing dishes, and weeding . . . ordinary things. There was a tension within me between the secular part of my life and the spiritual part. I often said that I wanted to go to heaven to be with God. Sometimes I meant that I wanted to see Him face to face, but most of the time what I was really thinking was, *I want to be released from the ordinary.*

Because of my responsibilities as wife and mother, I believed I couldn't pursue deep spirituality. The saying "How can I soar with the eagles when I'm stuck here with a bunch of turkeys?" described how I felt. How could I pray for hours like the great saints of God when I was so tired? How could I spend time in meditation when it was a luxury simply to have enough time to shave both legs in one sitting? In the confusion of trying to balance these two worlds in my mind, I was left drained and discouraged.

When I studied the character of God, I spent a year at a time meditating and studying each of the names for God which are covered in this book. As the years went by, I began to understand that God did not separate the secular from the sacred. I had always thought that eternity was something that awaited me at the end of life. After all, when I accepted Christ as my Savior I was told that I had received Him for eternity. I had always believed that death was the gateway to eternity.

But when I studied God's eternality, I sensed that there was something of great import that could change my life if I could only grasp it. Ecclesiastes 3:11 says, "He has also set eternity in the hearts of men." I wondered, *If eternity is in my heart, could it be that it is not "out there"—something that awaits me—but actually within me now? Could it be that I'm already living in eternity?* Further study led me to Hebrews 9:14 where I read that Christ, through "the eternal Spirit," offered Himself for our sin. I had accepted Christ as my personal Savior, and it became apparent to me that because He lived within my heart, I had eternity dwelling within me!

What does it mean for you and me that we are already living in eternity—that we don't have to wait until we get to heaven? Gently and lovingly, our great God showed me the ramifications of this awesome truth.

Everything Becomes Holy

God is working in eternity at the same time He works in our time. There are two planes, the eternal and the temporal, and they function simultaneously. Scripture makes it clear that God's ways are different from ours: "'For my thoughts are not your thoughts, neither are your ways my ways,' declares the LORD. 'As the heavens are higher than the earth, so are my ways higher than your ways and my thoughts than your thoughts'" (Isaiah 55:8-9). Neither is His time our time: "For a thousand years in your sight are like a day that has just gone by, or like a watch in the night" (Psalm 90:4). Habakkuk said in his prayer, "His ways are eternal" (Habakkuk 3:6). Because God has an eternal perspective, His ways are radically different from ours.

In his writings about time and eternity, Paul Tillich attempts to label the difference by referring to the "temporal now" and the "eternal now"[1] where one provides for the other. Tillich says, "There is not time *after* time, but there is eternity *above* time."[2] The fact that God dwells in eternity over time *and* dwells in us, concurrently, provides the believer with an opportunity to view life from a different perspective.

When we focus on the eternal—on the fact that God created time and is above it—by the help of the Spirit of God, we begin to link our time-boundedness to eternity, rather than separating the two. The secular and the spiritual are not two separate entities. God meant for us to live in harmony with both concepts.

What is the significance of this? The presence of God in a believer's life makes *everything* spiritual. When eternity dwells within you, your life is *not* ordinary because you house the Lord of Glory. Each moment, no matter how mundane, is infused with eternal spiritual significance. "There is an experience of the eternal breaking into time which transforms all life into a miracle of faith and action. Unspeakable, profound, and full of glory as an inward experience, it is the root of concern for all creation, the true ground of social endeavor."[3] This concept changed my thinking about my ordinary activities and everyday life!

When we understand that our daily lives are united with eternity, there is a settledness of soul. That is how God made us!

As this truth began to take root in my heart, I started to see that I could live intentionally, with purpose, in my little, out-of-the-way town. I did not need to go to the mission field or to have hours to spend each day in Bible study and prayer. My small children and tired husband were not a hindrance in my journey toward godliness; I began instead to see that they provided opportunities to let the great things of God be seen in the fabric of my daily life. My soul that had seemed so limited was now free.

In the book, *The Sacred Romance*, this wonder is called "a story big enough to live in."[4] You are not just a speck on a planet, but rather, a living temple of the Lord Most High. Nothing may have changed outwardly, but the light of God has come into your life and *everything* takes on a different perspective. I began realizing that this was the transformation of the soul. My soul was being awakened to the true "heavenly calling" (Hebrews 3:1) now on earth.

When eternity dwells within us, everything, whether mundane or not, takes on spiritual significance. We do not have to wait for eternity to start really living or to have deep intimacy with God. God has given us today. Every moment becomes significant because His presence is with us. Common everyday activities, including changing diapers or making a paper airplane for a little boy, become activities of eternal consequence because of the presence of the living God within.

The dilemma of the division between the sacred and the secular is also resolved. When we are totally God's, all we do and are is sacred. He is transforming our souls as we gain His perspective. The truth must "run in our blood and condition the complexion of our thoughts. We must practice living to the glory of God, actually and determinedly. . . . The knowledge that we are all God's, that He has received all and rejected nothing, will unify our inner lives and make *everything* sacred to us."[5]

We are commanded to do *"all* to the glory of God" (1 Corinthians 10:31, emphasis added). Both the sacred and the secular can bring God glory! The proof of godliness is not what we see on Sunday morning; rather, it is how we live, every day, in the mundane activities of life. If God is transforming us from the inside out, godliness will be found equally, both privately and publicly, and on Wednesday as well as on Sunday.

When God is our focus, everything we do is transformed by the Eternal One into the sacred. This truth was reinforced for me one time in the form of a gift of tamales given by a kind man of God.

I could hear the workmen repairing the street out in front of our home. Our little boy, Kurt, had joined the other neighborhood children to watch the exciting events taking place. Before long, Kurt came in carrying a tamale. As he handed it to me, he dutifully said, "The man told me to tell you that God loves you."

Of course, I followed Kurt back out to the street to find out who was the benefactor. I met an old man with a radiant face. In his broken English he told me that he had come to Christ late in life. He wanted to do something for God. One day he realized that he made good tamales. So each night he made tamales to pass out to the children that invariably came to watch the road repair he did by day. Each tamale was given with the same message: "God loves you." His simple message and gesture made an impact. God takes the ordinary of life and infuses it with His eternity, and the results are far greater than can be imagined.

The workman's message is for you. God loves you. Do you know this deep within your soul? Do you understand that God not only loves you today, He loves you for all eternity? As the Lover of your soul, your best interests are His. Every provision was made for you in the character of God. Every need that you will ever have is met in Him.

Do you know Him—*really* know Him?

Lord, Increase Our Speed

In this book we have only scratched the surface of who God is. The journey of knowing God takes an eternity. Our soul prospers in the process as we grow in the knowledge of the amazing God who loves us with a love that has no end.

If you truly want to be transformed, you must become preoccupied, engaged, absorbed, and engrossed with God, and allow that communion to do its work in your heart. When that happens, instead of a lifetime of soul thirst, you will come to know the Living Water. But remember, practicing holy habits is simply a way to help us keep preoccupied, engaged, absorbed, and engrossed in Him. So many things in our lives become meaningless rituals. Even good things—even holy habits. If the habit is the focus, rather than the Lord Himself, it will be of no transforming value. When you keep knowing God as the focus of all you do, He will change you from the inside out.

When you learn to let the forgiving, healing, sustaining work of God deal with your past and let His eternal love hold the hope of your future, you are free to enjoy His presence today. He takes the weight of yesterday and holds the fears of tomorrow. You can live with Him today. Each moment, no matter how mundane, becomes holy because God's presence fills it.

As you abide in Him, you will become like Him. He will teach you wisdom and contentment. You can trust Him to give you what you can handle, one moment at a time. Then you can face the many difficult questions of life with unshakable conviction. You have the freedom to live today lightheartedly because He is God and He has given you this moment in time.

One of the fathers of our faith, whose heart and attention were captured by God, was Gregory of Nyssa. He lived three hundred years after Christ. He was known for urging people toward a deeper relationship with God. His exhortation echoes down to us through the corridors of time: "You are competing admirably in the divine race. . . . Straining constantly for the prize of the heavenly calling, I exhort you, I urge you, I encourage you to increase your speed."[6]

Let us increase our speed toward knowing God and becoming like Him.

PRAYER

Holy Father, each time we get a glimpse of
another aspect of Your character,
You turn the page of our understanding and
we see that we have just begun our quest to know You.
Thank You for placing within us
the longing for intimacy with You,
for gently walking our finite minds into a deeper
awareness of You — the Infinite One.
For what we have been taught, we adore You.
Amen.

STUDY AND DISCUSSION QUESTIONS

1. In what ways have you separated the secular from the spiritual in your life?

2. What does the statement "The presence of God in a believer's life makes everything spiritual," mean to you?

3. How can you apply 1 Corinthians 10:31 in your life this week?

4. Read Psalm 139:17-18. How do you feel when you read these verses?

5. Read Psalm 36:7-9 and Psalm 65:4. Describe what happens to the soul that chooses to live in God's presence.

6. Hebrews 3:1 refers to a "heavenly calling." If God's transforming work in our lives is a part of that calling, what does the verse say that we need to do? How can you do that on a practical level?

7. "By the power of God, who has saved us and called us to a holy life—not because of anything we have done but because of his own purpose and grace. This grace was given us in Christ Jesus before the beginning of time . . ." (2 Timothy 1:8-9). What does this verse tell us about God's work in our lives? What does it tell us about God's time frame for that work?

8. Look through the twelve weeks of Bible study. Which week's lesson made the greatest impact on you? Write a letter to a friend, sharing the changes you have seen in your life because of what you learned.

9. Take your best stationary or buy a beautiful card. Write God a letter about some of the things you have learned about Him in this book. Store the letter with your valuables. Take time to give God praise for the insights you have gained.

10. If you are doing this study with a group, come prepared to share your letters with the group this week.

Recommended Reading List

When I was studying the character of God, I selected several books and studied each trait in all of the books. I wanted to understand different views of the attributes of God. I looked up every reference and then studied that reference in my favorite commentary. Here are some titles of books that have "increased my speed" on my journey toward knowing God better.

Commentaries

Barclay, William. *The Daily Study Bible Series.* Philadelphia, PA: Westminster Press, 1975. (Barclay's commentaries on the New Testament books of the Bible are rich because of the depth of background and insight he gives.)

Henry, Matthew. *Matthew Henry's Commentary on the Whole Bible.* McLean, VA: MacDonald Publishing Company, n.d. (This commentary has been very precious to me because it discusses each verse in the Bible in a devotional manner.)

God's Character
Bridges, Jerry. *The Joy of Fearing God.* Colorado Springs, CO: WaterBrook Press, 1997.

Needham, David. *Close to His Majesty.* Portland, OR: Multnomah Publishers, 1987.

Packer, J. I. *Knowing God.* Downers Grove, IL: InterVarsity Press, 1973.

Pink, Arthur. *The Attributes of God.* Grand Rapids, MI: Baker Book House, 1984.

Sheen, Fulton J. *Life of Christ.* New York, NY: Image Books, Doubleday Dell Publishing Group, Inc., 1977.

Tozer, A. W. *The Attributes of God.* Camp Hill, PA: Christian Publications, 1997.

Tozer, A. W. *The Knowledge of the Holy.* New York, NY: Harper & Row, 1961.

Names of God
Arthur, Kay. *Lord, I Want to Know You.* Old Tappan, NJ: Fleming H. Revell Company, 1984.

Stone, Nathan. *Names of God.* Chicago, IL: Moody Press, 1944.

God's Heart
The following books reveal the heart of God in various ways:

Carmichael, Amy. *Mimosa.* Fort Washington, PA: Christian Literature Crusade, The Dohnavur Fellowship, 1963.

Curtis, Brent and John Eldredge. *The Sacred Romance.* Nashville, TN: Thomas Nelson Publishers, 1997.

Nouwen, Henri J. M. *The Return of the Prodigal Son.* New York, NY: Image Books, Doubleday, 1994.

Richardson, Don. *Eternity in Their Hearts.* Ventura, CA: Regal Books, 1981.

Stowell, Joseph M. *Eternity.* Chicago, IL: Moody Press, 1995.

Prayer
(Any book about George Muller will show you how one man prayed faithfully and was changed in the process.)

Foster, Richard. *The Prayer Treasury.* New York, NY: Harper Collins Publishers, 1994.

Pierson, Arthur T. *George Muller of Bristol and His Witness to a Prayer-Hearing God.* New York, NY: Fleming H. Revell Company, n.d.

Steer, Roger. *George Muller Delighted in God!* Wheaton, IL: Harold Shaw Publishers, 1981.

White, John. *Daring to Draw Near.* Downers Grove, IL: Inter-Varsity Press, 1977. (This book helped mold my thinking about ten of the great prayers in the Bible.)

Our Response to God

Bridges, Jerry. *The Practice of Godliness.* Colorado Springs, CO: NavPress, 1984.

De Caussade, Jean-Pierre. *The Sacrament of the Present Moment.* New York, NY: HarperCollins, 1989. (This book provides a great view of what happens to the soul as it begins to see each day in light of eternity.)

Dillow, Linda. *Calm My Anxious Heart.* Colorado Springs, CO: NavPress, 1998.

Foster, Richard and James Bryan Smith, eds. *Devotional Classics.* San Francisco, CA: HarperCollins Publishers, 1989.

George, Elizabeth. *Loving God with All Your Mind.* Eugene, OR: Harvest House Publishers, 1994.

Gibbs, A. P. *Worship.* Kansas City, KS: Walter Inc., n.d.

Lawrence, Brother. *The Practice of the Presence of God.* Springdale, PA: Whitaker House, 1982.

Lewis, C. S. *Mere Christianity.* New York, NY: Macmillan Publishing Company, 1943.

Miller, Edward. *Letters to the Thirsty.* Colorado Springs, CO: WaterBrook Press, 1998.

Pink, Arthur. *The Doctrine of Sanctification.* Swengel, PA: Bible Truth Depot, 1955.

Pusey, E. B., compiled by Mary W. Tileston. *Daily Strength for Daily Needs.* England: Messers, Samson, Low & Company, 1928.

Taylor, Dr. and Mrs. Howard. *Hudson Taylor's Spiritual Secret.* Chicago, IL: Moody Press, n.d.

Tozer, A. W. *The Pursuit of God.* Camp Hill, PA: Christian Publications, 1982.

Tozer, A. W. *The Size of the Soul.* Camp Hill, PA: Christian Publications, 1992.

Notes

Chapter 1
* While the content of this book reflects the insights and experiences of both Shelly Cook Volkhardt and Mimi Wilson, this book is written in Mimi's voice in order to avoid confusion.
1. Oswald Chambers, *My Utmost for His Highest* (Uhrichsville, OH: Barbour and Company, Inc., 1963), p. 134.

Chapter 2
1. David Needham, *Close to His Majesty* (Portland, OR: Multnomah Publishers, 1987), pp. 36, 37.
2. Kay Arthur, *Lord, I Want to Know You* (Old Tappan, NJ: Fleming H. Revell Company, 1984), p. 21.
3. Don Richardson, *Eternity in Their Hearts* (Ventura, CA: Regal Books, 1981), pp. 31–32.
4. Sharon Begley, "Science Finds God," *Newsweek*, CXXXII, no. 4, 27 July 1998, p. 44.
5. Begley, p. 44.
6. Begley, p. 42.
7. John Patterson, as quoted by William Barclay in *The Daily Study Bible Series Gospel of John*, vol. 1 (Philadelphia, PA: The Westminster Press, 1975), p. 27.
8. Matthew Henry, *Matthew Henry's Commentary on the Whole Bible* (Grand Rapids, MI: Guardian Press, 1976), p. 158.

9. "Prayers for the Natural Order," *The Book of Common Prayer*, Number 40, according to the use of The Episcopal Church (The Seabury Press, September 1979), p. 827.

10. William R. Newcott, "Worlds Without End," *National Geographic*, 191, no. 4, April 1997, p. 11.

Chapter 3

1. Robert Young, *Young's Literal Translation of the Holy Bible Revised Edition* (Grand Rapids, MI: Baker Book House, 1953), p. 2.

2. As quoted by William R. Bright, "The Van Dusen Letter" (Arrowhead Springs, San Bernadino, CA: Campus Crusade for Christ, 1965), p. 2.

3. William Barclay, *The Daily Study Bible, Letters of James and Peter* (Philadelphia, PA: The Westminster Press, 1960), p. 188.

4. Tony Evans, *Our God Is Awesome* (Chicago, IL: Moody Publishers, 1994), pp. 75, 78.

5. Jerry Bridges, *The Pursuit of Holiness* (Colorado Springs, CO: NavPress, 1982), pp. 31-32.

6. R. C. Sproul, *The Holiness of God* (Chicago, IL: Tyndale House Publishers, 1987), p. 233.

7. Andrew Murray, *The Deeper Christian Life* (Grand Rapids, MI: Francis Asbury Press of Zondervan Publishing House, 1985), p. 104.

8. A.W. Tozer, *The Knowledge of the Holy* (San Francisco, CA: HarperSanFrancisco, 1961), p. 38.

Chapter 4

1. Oswald Chambers, *My Utmost for His Highest* (Uhrichsville, OH: Barbour and Company, Inc., 1963), p. 136.

2. "Amazing Grace" by John Newton. *Praise! Our Songs and Hymns* (Grand Rapids, MI: Singspiration Music, 1979), p. 293.

3. CoMission, "The Chariot" Newsletter, Volume 2, Issue 1, First Quarter 1995.

4. John Blanchard, *Truth for Life: A Devotional Commentary on the Epistle of James* (Welwyn, Hertfordshire, England: Evangelical Press, 1986), p. 268.

5. H. E. Manning, as quoted in *Daily Strength for Daily Needs*, compiled by Mary W. Tileston (England: Messers, Samson, Low & Company, 1928), p. 18.

Chapter 5
1. Amy Carmichael, *Mimosa* (Fort Washington, PA: Christian Literature Crusade, 1963), p. 11.
2. Carmichael, p. 55.
3. A. W. Tozer, *The Pursuit of God* (Harrisburg, PA: Christian Publications, Inc., 1982), p. 50.
4. Dallas Willard, *The Divine Conspiracy* (San Francisco, CA: HarperSanFrancisco, 1998), p. 67.
5. George A. Butterick, as quoted by Richard Foster and James Bryan Smith, eds., in *Devotional Classics* (San Francisco, CA: HarperCollins Publishers, 1989), p. 103.
6. James Borst, as quoted by Richard Foster in *The Prayer Treasury* (New York, NY: HarperCollins Publishers, 1994), p. 163.

Chapter 6
1. George MacDonald, *Annals of a Quiet Neighborhood* (Philadelphia, PA: David McKay, Publisher, n.d.), p. 203.

Chapter 7
1. Nathan Stone, *Names of God* (Chicago, IL: Moody Press, 1944), p. 85.
2. Stone, pp. 86–87.
3. Lester Sumrall, *The Names of God: God's Character Revealed Through His Names* (New Kensington, PA: Whitaker House, 1993), p.114.
4. Stone, p. 93.
5. Matthew Henry, *Matthew Henry's Commentary on the Whole Bible* (McLean, VA: MacDonald Publishing Company, 1976), p. 1139.
6. A. W. Tozer, *The Knowledge of the Holy* (San Francisco, CA: HarperSanFrancisco, 1961), p. 93.

Chapter 8
1. Nathan Stone, *Names of God* (Chicago, IL: Moody Press, 1944), p. 117.
2. Frank E. Gaebelein, *The Expositor's Bible Commentary*, vol. 3 (Grand Rapids, MI: Zondervan Publishing Company, 1992), p. 420.
3. Stone, p. 113.

Chapter 9

1. William Barclay, *The Daily Study Bible, The Gospel of Mark* (Edinburgh, Scotland: The Saint Andrew Press, 1991), p. 10.
2. William Barclay, *The Daily Study Bible, The Letter to the Hebrews* (Edinburg, Scotland: The Saint Andrew Press, 1963), p. 98.
3. Matthew Henry, *Matthew Henry's Commentary on the Whole Bible*, vol. VI (McLean, VA: MacDonald Publishing Company, n.d.), p. 923.
4. Barclay, *The Daily Study Bible, The Letter to the Hebrews*, p. 102.
5. Brennan Manning, *The Ragamuffin Gospel* (Sisters, OR: Multnomah Books, 1990), p. 97.
6. Alice Poynor, "The Exchanged Life," *The Discipleship Journal, Holiness*, January/February 1989, p. 32.
7. Poynor, p. 32.
8. A. P. Gibbs, *Worship—The Christian's Highest Occupation* (Denver, CO: Reprinted by the Wilson Foundation, n.d.), p. 15.
9. A. W. Tozer, *The Pursuit of God* (Camp Hill, PA: Christian Publishing Inc., 1982), p. 127.
10. Richard J. Foster and James Bryan Smith, *Devotional Classics* (San Francisco, CA: HarperSanFrancisco, 1993), p. 147.
11. Jerry Bridges, "Declaration of Dependence," *The Discipleship Journal, Holiness*, January/February, 1989, p. 29.
12. Richard Foster, *Prayer Treasury* (New York, NY: Prince Press, reprinted by permission of HarperCollins, 1994), p. 100.

Chapter 10

1. Told by Becky Pippert at Urbana 1980 in a plenary session. Sent to me by Dave Pavey.
2. *The New Dictionary of Thoughts*, compiled by Tyron Edwards, D.D. (Standard Book Company, 1963), p. 348.
3. Edwards, p. 262.
4. Charles L. Wallis, ed., *The Treasure Chest* (New York, NY: Harper and Row, 1965), p. 65.
5. Wallis, p. 25.
6. Douglas Burton-Christie, "Into the Labyrinth: Walking the Way of Wisdom," *Weavings, A Journal of the Christian Spiritual Life*, Volume XII, Number 4, July/August 1997, Nashville, TN, p. 24.
7. Burton-Christie, p. 25.
8. Joseph M. Stowell, "Credentials or Character?" Front Lines, *Moody Monthly*, Volume 95, Number 3, November 1994, p. 4.

9. A.W. Tozer, *The Knowledge of the Holy* (New York, NY: Harper & Row, 1961), p. 66.
10. J.I. Packer, *Knowing God* (Downers Grove, IL: InterVarsity Press, 1973), p. 80.
11. Richard Foster, *Prayer Treasury* (New York, NY: HarperCollins, 1992), p. 153.
12. Tozer, p. 68.

Chapter 11

1. William Barclay, *The Letters to Timothy, Titus and Philemon* (Edinburgh, Scotland: Saint Andrews Press, 1991), p. 128.
2. William Barclay, *The Letters to the Philippians, Colossians, and Thessalonians*, rev. ed. (Philadelphia, PA: The Westminster Press, 1976), p. 85.
3. Barclay, *The Letters to Timothy, Titus and Philemon*, p. 129.
4. E. B. Pusey, compiled by Mary W. Tileston, *Daily Strength for Daily Needs* (England: Messers, Samson, Low & Company, 1928), p. 144.

Chapter 12

1. F. Forrester Church, ed., *The Essential Tillich, An Anthology of the Writings of Paul Tillich* (New York: Macmillan Publishing Company, 1987), p. 127.
2. Church, p. 123.
3. Thomas R. Kelly, *A Testament of Devotion* (San Francisco, CA: HarperSanFrancisco, 1996), p. 65.
4. Brent Curtis and John Eldredge, *The Sacred Romance* (Nashville, TN: Thomas Nelson Publishers, 1997), p. 35.
5. A. W. Tozer, *The Pursuit of God* (Camp Hill, PA: Christian Publications, Inc., 1982), p. 122.
6. Gregory of Nyssa, as quoted by, Richard J. Foster and James Bryan Smith, in *Devotional Classics* (San Francisco, CA: HarperSanFrancisco, 1993), p. 155.

About the Authors

Mimi Wilson

MIMI WILSON grew up in the Ituri Forest in Africa with her missionary parents. She went to study nursing in Colorado, where she met her husband. Mimi's husband, Cal Wilson, practiced private medicine for ten years before they went to Ecuador, where they served the Lord for nine years. Mimi has written two books, the best-selling *Once-A-Month Cooking* and *Table Talk*. Cal and Mimi have three children and two grandchildren. They live in Colorado.

Shelly Cook Volkhardt

SHELLY COOK VOLKHARDT grew up in Taiwan. She studied at Biola University where she met her husband, Glen. Shelly is a Bible teacher. The Volkhardts were missionaries in Ecuador for twenty years. They currently live in Miami and are assigned to the Latin America Region. They have two sons.